THE QUALITY PLAN

Practical Advice to Keep Claims Clients Coming Back

KEVIN M. QUINLEY, CPCU

Claims Books

SEATTLE, WASH.

The Quality Plan:
Practical Advice to Keep Claims Clients Coming Back
by Kevin M. Quinley, CPCU

© Copyright 1992
Claims Books,
a division of IW Publications
1001 Fourth Avenue Plaza
Suite 3029
Seattle, Washington 98154

ISBN 0-9634957-0-4
Library of Congress Catalog Card Number: 92-75834

Manufactured in the United States of America
First Edition

table of contents

acknowledgements

Academy Award winners drone on and on mercilessly, thanking everyone in a tiresome manner which has become a virtual parody. I will strive not to repeat this error.

In this less august forum, I wish to thank those people who have helped move this book from concept to actuality. Some of them I have never met in person, but their thoughts and writings have influenced me — positively I believe — and profoundly. For helping me with insights on the topic of customer and client service, I wish to thank Tom Peters (The Tom Peters Group), Fred Poppe (Poppe Tyson, Inc.), Gail Roppo (Crawford & Company), Charles Caronia (Caronia Corporation), John Nelson (Countrywide Services Corporation), and Ray Waters and David Bauer (GAB Business Services).

I owe a debt of gratitude toward my clients, who continually give me refresher courses on customer service.

Special thanks go to Bill Thorness, Doug Canfield and Claims Books, who encouraged this project along.

This book would not have been possible either without the sacrifice of my wife Jane and my two sons, who put up with a temperamental and preoccupied writer during the course of this project. They have taught me a thing or two about service, and it is to them that I dedicate this book.

K.M.Q.
Fairfax, Va., May 1992

Introduction

"Unfortunately, the subject of how-to-provide great service brings countless experts out of the woodwork. I say 'unfortunately' because service is much easier to talk about than to accomplish."
— John L. Nelson, Countrywide Services
Corporation, St. Louis, Missouri

"Twilight Zone" fans will recall one memorable episode when aliens from outer space landed in America with a cryptic text, "To Serve Man." Everyone was charmed by the aliens' approach, and some humans even elected to enter the alien spacecraft to visit their home planet. One small problem: the book itself was written in some indecipherable tongue, an alien dialect, no doubt. No one could decipher more than the seemingly innocuous title of the book. As the humans were ascending the gangplank that would seal them inside the Martian spacecraft, one excited man ran up beneath the craft, having cracked the code. He had translated "To Serve Man." As the door to the spacecraft closed, he screamed, "IT'S A COOKBOOK!"

This is a book on how to serve clients. It is not a cookbook. As a service business, however, much of the claims industry is in its own "twilight zone." When one thinks of service excellence, like it or not, the insurance and claim fields do not leap to mind. Ask most people what they think of insurance companies or claim

1

adjusting services, and they are likely to stick out their tongues or hold their noses. Some people think the service stinks! The litany of complaints can glaze the eyes: slow contacts, unreturned phone calls, unanswered correspondence, indifference, failure to report or communicate, not following directions, not keeping promises, not taking the time needed to do the job right, not paying enough. And so on and so on.

We labor under a yoke of poor public image. Consider, simply as one example, the following doggerel from an attorney who makes his living suing insurers:

> *His wife and children left him.*
> *He's banished from his club.*
> *Sam, the village barman,*
> *Won't serve him in the pub.*
> *His business colleagues scorn him.*
> *His dreams are on the shelf.*
> *But let us note, in fairness,*
> *He brought it on himself.*
> *He broke his code of honor.*
> *He had no sense of shame,*
> *For he was in insurance*
> *And he went and paid a claim.*

—Eugene R. Anderson
Anderson Kill Olick & Oshinsky
(*Risk Management,* March 1992)

Unfortunately, the book "In Search of Excellence" contained not one example drawn from the insurance or claims adjusting industries. The Malcolm Baldridge Award, given annually to American businesses with top-notch quality, has never been awarded to an insurance company, much less a claims adjusting service.

When business writers periodically reach for examples of excellence, they mention Nordstrom, Stew Leonard's grocery store and Federal Express. They never seem to mention adjusting companies. It is not altogether uncommon for large buyers of outside adjusting services — large self-insureds — to play "musical adjusters," periodically hiring then discharging provider after provider, striving to find a right match. Larger companies are increasingly bringing in-house the role of claims handling, seeking more control and reduced costs. Often, these decisions to bring the adjusting function in-house are service driven; that is to say, poor service has driven the business away from outside claim service providers and into the corporation. Hence, some adjusters and claim service providers run the risk of working themselves into extinction through mediocre service, becoming the claims equivalent of the dodo bird.

There are, however, a few exceptions. Some insurers fare well on a "service honor roll" on the property/casualty side, notably United Services Automobile Association and Amica Mutual Insurance Company. The head of USAA, based in San Antonio, Texas, says "Insurance companies don't have an image problem. They have a reality problem." Could the same be true for claim departments and adjusting companies? Could it be that adjusters — and adjusting companies employing them — do not have so much of an image problem as a reality problem?

Those of us in the claims industry lament our image. We strive to overcome a negative image. Some say that adjusters are right up (or down) there with bill collectors and used car salesmen on the esteem scale. Others consider the claims department as the ghetto of the insurance industry. Others have suggested anatomical, if not scatological, metaphors for the claim department's role. Is it an image problem or is it, in part, a reality problem?

Work on reality, and image will change. Improve service, and the image of insurance companies, claim adjusters and outside adjusting firms will improve as well. This book aims to change what may have become a reality problem for claim departments and claim services. We have become accustomed to certain levels of service which suit us just fine, but may or may not suit our clients. We may be driven more by our own need for convenience than by our client's needs.

In our rush to get investigations completed, to close files, and to bill time, we have sometimes seen our clients as a nuisance and distraction rather than the lifeblood of our image and business. We are so preoccupied with the mechanics of our own business within the loss adjustment field that we do not take the time to learn about our clients' businesses, their concerns, their worries or their wants. In our accumulation of technical expertise in mastering areas of claims adjustment, we are tempted to look down on the client's questions or complaints with the notion, "That idiot does not know what he — or she — is talking about!"

In our race to adjust, investigate and settle claims, we too often view policyholders and clients as distractions, interruptions or problems which need to be solved. We rarely see them as people who need our attention. We often spend our energies trying to do the right job instead of considering whether we're doing the job right. Just as most businesses cannot afford to ignore their customers' needs for long, neither can adjusters.

Clients are concerned about adjusting costs. But some might be willing to swallow those costs easier if they received better service from outside adjusting companies. Commenting on what drives clients crazy, Charles Caronia, president of Caronia Corporation (Melville, New York) states, "Cost is mentioned, but it's not a prime factor. In fact, if costs become critical issues, then that's a sign that something is fundamentally wrong." The biggest client sore point, he feels, is "failure to provide consistent work product, which is often a function of staff turnover or excessive caseloads. Somebody leaves and is not replaced for months, if at all."

Customer loyalty still exists, but it is a dying breed. Clients no longer tolerate complacency. Fewer businesses will keep accounts with outside service providers simply on the force of historical inertia. Every outside service provider gets a fresh look — both in terms of price and quality. Fail to adequately service a client's account this year, and you may find this is the last year you have it. Studies have shown that it costs much more to get new business than it does to keep existing accounts. Hence, while independent adjusting firms should strive to develop new business sources, they must not overlook the obvious: they need to serve their existing clients well. We cannot think the job is done once we sign on a company as a client.

There is an apocryphal story about a risk manager who died and was told by St. Peter that he could choose heaven or hell, but first had to spend one day in each. After a pleasant but quiet day in heaven, the risk manager visited hell. There, a wild party was in progress. Everyone came up to the risk manager, befriended him, offered him drinks and made him the object of attention. The music played and the risk manager had a fun time. Returning to St. Peter, the risk manager said, "I know this is gonna' sound crazy, but I had a great time, and I'll pick hell." And off to hell he went. But the place he returned to was nothing like the place he had just partied at. The place was dark, uncomfortably hot and stank of sulfur. The people who had been his buddies the day before ignored him and walked right past. Finally, the risk manager was able to track down one of the people he had seen at the party the day before. "What's going on here?" he asked. "Yesterday there was a party, music, drinks and lots of friendly people." "Oh," the person replied, "that was different — yesterday you were a prospect. Today, you're a CLIENT!"

Once we win business, do we feel that our job is done? Businesses of all kinds are now re-discovering that, if they want customer loyalty, they must not only meet but exceed their clients' expectations for good service. Good service is easy to discuss in the abstract. It is harder to define, but specific real-life examples help. There are a few well-recognized "models" of companies which deliver superior, Gold Standard service. In our quest for models of good service, insurers and claim professionals must be willing to look to other businesses — wholly different types of enterprises — for example and inspiration.

5

In Ann Arbor, Michigan some people had the radical idea that if you could deliver a hot, tasty pizza in a half-hour or less, you could build a successful business. Domino's Pizza is now a multi-billion dollar business. They have a very simple idea, but take incredible pains to execute it. Any idea in any business which satisfies client needs is never silly. Your clients may be customers of a business that cares about service, whether its L.L. Bean, American Express or the Four Seasons Hotel chain.

You may not be expected to deliver settlement checks or close files in thirty minutes or less. Your claim offices may not need to build drive-thru windows for claimants and policyholders to pick up their settlement checks. However, a client may very well expect you to complete a car appraisal in 48 hours after assignment, or contact a policyholder or claimant within 24 hours after an assignment. Such clients are likely to ask themselves, "If a mail order retailer, hotel or credit card company cares about my business, why won't my adjusting service even return my phone calls?"

Does it really make sense to compare a claims adjustment service to a hotel or pizza delivery chain? In some ways yes and in some ways no. Adjusters, always striving for professionalism, may be loathe to place themselves in the same category as pizza delivery-persons or retail sales persons. Maybe. However, the lessons of superior service, found in whatever quarter, should not be lost on adjusters, claim departments, or independent claim services. The claims adjusting profession can certainly learn from other businesses which focus on customer satisfaction. In the past, the adjuster-client relationship flowed through a very skewed system, with often limited need for client or policyholder participation.

Today's business environment, however, has given customers a new sense of empowerment. Increasingly, clients are refusing to tolerate a one-sided business relationship with their insurance carriers and, by extension, with their insurer's claims department or outside adjusting firm. To an extent, clients are increasingly concluding that their claims are too important to be left to claim adjusters, insurers or independent claim offices. This is the day of the assertive consumer. Clients will not stand by passively as the proverbial "potted plant," while their claims are being adjusted. Clients have learned — often the hard way — that effective claim systems do not run on auto-pilot. Clients are going to jump into the fray, get involved, make suggestions, question decisions, offer input. Claims are high-profile matters, and one sensitive claim mishandled by an adjusting company can negatively impact a client's business and reputation. Thus, companies and clients are increasingly likely to be more and more demanding of adjusting services. The "good old days" of "Here is a new assignment — please handle to conclusion" are largely a thing of the past.

Claim assignments are no exception to this trend. Clients may not know everything there is to know about claims. They may not know as much as you do in the technical aspects of adjusting claims. The client does, however, know what he or she does NOT like. Studies show that very few dissatisfied customers ever actually complain. Instead, they simply take their business elsewhere.

Burned by past experiences and misadventures with adjusting services, they are disillusioned at going out and hiring an adjuster who:

- Has no experience, expertise or interest in the client's business
- Is more obsessed with her caseload, and getting it down, than with handling each case on its merits
- May be more likely to treat the client's claims as crates on a loading dock rather than rare antiques. The challenge from the newest adjuster trainee to the vice president of claims is to use this empowerment mood as an opportunity for success in a highly competitive business climate.

Businesses measure satisfaction by contacting customers after the sale. They ask if anything could be improved. They contact their customers periodically to see if they are still satisfied. It is simple: How did our staff handle your phone calls? What did you think of the fees you were charged? You begin to form a picture — like it or not — of how clients perceive your adjusting service. Many busy claim people and services find this contact system difficult, but it is simple and it works. The very fact that your adjusting service stays in touch with its clients sends signals of care and concern for clients' well-being.

Reaching out to clients may provide some eye-opening information on how clients evaluate adjusters and adjusting services. Policyholders, insurance company claim examiners and risk managers look for adjusters and adjusting services who:

- Keep them informed of the progress of their cases or claims
- Show genuine interest and concern about client problems
- Charge fair and reasonable rates
- Report promptly and regularly
- Are prompt in all matters
- Explain the claims process
- Have strong work habits

Please note: these points do not include any reference to missing brilliance or intellect. Clients expect their adjusters and adjusting services to be technically proficient in damage estimating, legal liability assessment, investigative techniques and negotiating skills. They also expect some understanding. Clients and customers may base more of their choices on the "package of values" that you bring with your claim file solutions.

Many adjusters and claim professionals believe that clients do not know what they want, and do not appreciate what they get. While this may be true, clients do know when they are less than happy. Clients are no longer passive bystanders in a caveat emptor world. They want to be active players in the process of managing their claims. If you listen to clients and act on what you have heard, you have just made clients part of the decision-making process. However, if you fail at this process, clients will likely take their assignments and business elsewhere. That is why state of the art claim services MUST solicit client feedback.

No one model of service can ever hope to capture all that it takes to satisfy clients. You cannot wish your busy claim staff or firm into a client/customer satisfaction program. It must come from the bottom up — not the top down. It must come from the adjusters and staff who commit themselves to quality client care. This requires a new model and an understanding of how to communicate.

Client service is an acquired skill. Everyone who works in the claims industry needs it. There should be constant pressure to improve service. Gaining and keeping clients' allegiance is just good business. This book is for:

- Insurance company claim personnel
- Independent adjusting companies
- In-house claim professionals who work for self-insureds

This book is aimed at everyone in the claims hierarchy and organizational chart, from the newest telephone adjuster to the vice president of claims. Keeping clients happy is hard, yet it is deceptively simple. Find out what the client wants and likes. Give it to them just that way. Pay attention to the details. Keep your promises. Follow up. Solicit feedback — critical as well as laudatory.

This book presents over 100 ways to keep clients happy and to hang on to the clients you have. If clients are happy, we all prosper. To an extent, it is a way to seek, and maintain, a competitive advantage vis a vis other insurers and claim services. By following the suggestions herein, you will set yourself apart from 99 percent of your competition. If clients are happy, you get business. You get more business. You get your bills paid. You acquire a word-of-mouth following which no advertising budget could buy.

You can read these chapters in the sequence offered, but each one can be sampled and utilized on a stand-alone basis. Service is easier to discuss than to deliver, but let's take a look at the building blocks of good client claim service ...

Communications

It really doesn't matter how good a job you do in handling claims if you don't communicate with your clients. You must communicate with them and, occasionally, even toot your own horn. Adjusters and claim professionals — and their employers — can easily get so immersed in handling claims that they neglect to communicate with their clients. No hard data is available, but from my discussions with clients I would hazard to say that communication — or lack thereof — is the number one complaint which clients lodge against their claim service firms. You can rarely go wrong by being overly communicative. Here are some practical tips on how to improve your communications with clients.

Seven Steps to a
Good First Impression

Here are seven ways to improve the first impression you and your office make on clients, visitors and prospects:

1. **Be image conscious, not image obsessed.** Find out what kind of image appeals to your clients. Some expect opulent offices and appointments. Others want a bare-bones outfit, with low overhead translating into lower costs. Do you understand what makes clients pick your adjusting service and return there, file after file, assignment after assignment? If not, find out. This is key information in cementing and building a clientele, whether you are a Mom and Pop adjusting outfit or a large nationwide third-party administrator.

2. **Be professional and look the part.** Do your office areas and your personnel project the image that you want? Do they reflect your success as a claims operation and demonstrate that yours is a well-organized and effective adjusting service? Do you, your professional staff and support staff dress to convey the image you want to convey? All of these non-verbal cues send messages — good or bad — to visiting clients.

3. **Make waiting short and comfortable.** Is it comfortable to wait in your office? How long is the wait for visitors? Believe it or not, the time of clients, claimants and policyholders is valuable

too. Everybody, especially clients, expect you to be punctual. Are the seats comfortable? Is there reading material available? Does the receptionist ask them if they would like a cup of coffee or soda? Become a student of your clients' preferences, whether it be in reading or refreshment. Sweat the details!

4. **Empower front-line personnel.** Make sure your staff's manners and actions reassure clients and build their confidence in your adjusting service. Make sure clients are treated like royalty while they wait to talk with you by phone or in person. Public relations often begins with that $7-an-hour receptionist or telephone operator. When a client arrives, the front-line people should lay on the big smile and treat the visitor like a VIP. This may require some planning and prior briefing.

5. **Use conference rooms.** Clients should expect your claims office to be well-organized and professional looking. A conference room, because it is easier to keep neat and clean, may be a better place to meet than a paper-strewn office. If the conference room has been used recently for someone's workroom or for a meeting, check to make sure it is tidy and check it regularly for neatness.

6. **Clear the files.** When a client visits your office, keep your desk or conference room table clear of files. If you must have files at hand — and that is often a good idea — avoid piling the files on the desk or the floor. Try a credenza.

7. **Make professionalism a team effort.** Enlist the help of all claim staff — support staff and professional, from the file clerk to the claims manager — to keep the entire office as neat and orderly as possible. There are always claim files which can be put away, extraneous paper which can be discarded and shelves which can be straightened.

Make sure that your office and work quarters — along with your business attire — are "dressed for success" to project a positive, professional image to clients.

Keeping Up With Clients

Keep plugged in to the trade publications which your client is reading. Any adjuster or claims professional touting itself as specializing in casualty claims work ought to subscribe to and read:

- *The National Underwriter*
- *Business Insurance*
- *Claims*

Some adjusting firms already do. You can get a tremendous amount of information about your client just by reading the trade press. It doesn't hurt, either, to let the client know that you are keeping abreast of what's happening. This is a way to signal to clients that you are interested in them, in their business and understand the larger context into which their business fits. The following are examples of bits of news where a brief note from the adjuster to the client would be appreciated:

- A trade publication ranks the client as among the top ten in its field.
- A special service honor which the client company wins.
- The client is profiled in the "Companies to Watch" feature in *Fortune* magazine.
- An investment magazine touts the client company stock as one of the best values in the market.

- *Inc.* magazine names the client company as one of the top 100 entrepreneurial companies in America.
- The financial pages show second quarter earnings are at a record level.
- The *Wall Street Journal* "On the Street" column cites the stock as a superb value.
- A key promotion occurs within the claims or risk management department.

The adjuster can mention this in passing, place a phone call, drop a hand-written note — anything to telegraph to the client that you understand their business. Ingratiating? Maybe. But it shows the client that you are interested in them, in their business and that you pay attention. A little bit of such attention will elevate you and your adjusting firm above the competition.

Keeping Up
With Reports

The number one reason clients fire their adjusting services is failure to report. If a client has specific guidelines for reporting, whether it is every 30, 60 or 90 days, abide by those time frames religiously.

Make absolutely sure that you send engagement letters, status reports, copies of documents and correspondence to clients. It is simply a good habit to stay in touch. Tell the client at the start of the claim assignment that they can expect to hear from you or other members of the claim department regularly, or that you will notify them if delays arise. Try to introduce the client to other people in the claims department who can answer their questions when you are not available. Make sure there is a communication and follow-up system with little chance for break-downs. If a client does not specify reporting guidelines, ASK THEM how often they want reports.

If a client does not give you a guideline, impose one on yourself anyway.

Make sure that you maintain personal contact with your clients while their claims are open. Consider making periodic telephone calls to them during the active phases of a claim and consider regular face-to-face meetings if you have a substantial caseload. Regular status reports will keep clients current on their claim files, and facilitate client-vendor discussions. If you have or can develop a loss prevention checklist to help them avoid future claims, you have provided a value-added service.

Clients cannot manage claims without information. When a case is open with a financial reserve, clients cannot get that information without periodic and meaningful reports from the adjuster.

It has always amazed me what a problem this is with some adjusters, however. One would think that picking up a dictaphone mike, talking into a machine and billing for this time would be one of the easiest parts of a claim professional's job.

Tell the client what is happening with his case. If nothing is happening, do NOT ignore the client's request or guidelines because nothing is happening. If nothing is happening on a case, tell the client that nothing is happening.

Tell the client WHY nothing is happening.

If the fact that nothing happening is GOOD for the client, explain why.

Be prepared to explain why YOU shouldn't be making something happen. Is nothing happening on a case because the adjuster is not working on the case?

Claim departments answer to many different and outside constituencies, so it is vital that their files reflect proper documentation on the status of litigated files. It is not because of any paper fetish that clients want reports. The client and its files are evaluated by many inside and outside constituencies. To name a few:

- the risk manager or financial VP
- reinsurers
- policyholders
- excess and umbrella carriers
- auditors
- actuaries

Failing to report to clients compromises their ability to manage claims and to know what is happening. It also makes clients look bad in the eyes of those who evaluate their work. Cardinal rule of business: never make the customer look bad.

Let the customer know what is happening on the case. Review diary and tickler systems within the claims department to ensure that files are reported on a regular basis. This way, you should never received one of the letters which begin, "We have not heard from you in four months, so please ..."

Late reporting and non-reporting drives clients crazy. Like a red light on a car's dashboard, it is one warning sign of deteriorating service. More than high bills, it may be the number one reason why adjusting services get fired.

Stay in touch.

Informing Clients
About Claim Developments

Clients look to you to know and apply the existing adjusting regulations to their particular claim or loss. Clients rarely are fascinated by claims for their intrinsic value. In this they may differ from many adjusters. To the insurance client, the process of handling claims is a means to an end. That end is to close their file or solve their problem. They are very busy and are not necessarily interested in a blow-by-blow description of a case. They ARE interested in the bottom-line impact such a case has on their business.

It is up to you to keep the client updated as to legal developments in their field, whether it be automobile liability, slip and falls, medical malpractice, bad faith, product liability or uninsured motorist losses.

At minimum, this means updating the client, whether in the form of a newsletter, a circular or merely a letter discussing a new development. Clients are interested in knowing the results of:

- Key court and appellate decisions affecting their operations.
- Pending, proposed or recent statute changes which affect them (tort reform, etc.).

- Results of recent jury trial and settlements which might help them establish "going rates" for various types of injuries and claims.
- Changes in workers compensation procedures and benefit levels.

The important thing to remember is to translate the legal and insurance mumbo jumbo into language the client will understand. More important, perhaps, translate the court holding into a distilled set of practical "do's" and "don'ts" for clients.

Understandably, there is a reluctance to offer legal advice via newsletter. Lawyers do not want to be sued for malpractice because of advice given by newsletter, or they may want the newsletter to serve as a "teaser" to attract more business. Practice of law by lay adjusters is verboten. Short of giving legal advice, however, the adjusting company's client newsletter can offer practical tips on reporting, investigating and preventing claims.

The adjusting firm which can not only report on developments in the law but who can translate this into practical advice for clients will rise head and shoulders above the competition. Too often, clients get frustrated because the adjusters either do not give specific usable advice ("It depends ...") or they equivocate so much as to make the advice useless.

Informing Clients About Your Firm

Let clients know if your adjusting firm or claims department has added staff with expertise which can be brought to bear on insurance work.

If you are going on vacation for two or more weeks, consider letting clients know. Adjusters need vacations, perhaps more than many other professionals. They need time to decompress. This increases their effectiveness as claim professionals. However, don't have your secretary tell clients or callers that you "stepped away from your desk" when in fact you are in Bermuda for a few weeks on vacation!

The same goes for time when you are tied up on a special out-of-town project — like a hurricane loss — for weeks. Clients understand that you DO have other cases and clients, but they will be ticked if they are told, "He's not in right now," when you're not going to be in for weeks.

Let your client know in advance if you are going to be inaccessible for a while, whether it is due to vacation, Army reserve duty, sabbatical or elective surgery. This is not only good business, but common courtesy. Let the client know in advance which other adjuster(s) will be covering for you during your absence.

If you change companies and approach the client of your

former firm for business, better be prepared to answer the following questions or — better yet — volunteer the information without having been asked:

- Why you made the jump to another adjusting firm or to form a new firm?
- Why your new adjusting company is qualified and well-suited to handle the client's cases?
- How does your cost and fee structure compare? Many times adjusters leave big firms for smaller firms, or form their own small boutique adjusting outfit. Clients are often dismayed that the presumed economies of scale — which are paraded out as a reason for the adjuster leaving the big bloated company — do not seem to translate into lower hourly fees or costs.

Don't be afraid to toot your own horn a bit:

- Successful claim denials you have had sustained recently.
- Professional or trade journal articles you have written and have had published.
- Presentations you have made recently on topics germane to the client.

Think again about sending around those engraved announcements that Brad Barrister has just been named partner with The Firm. If I do not know Mr. Barrister, I will likely toss this announcement in the circular file. Save printing costs and postage.

Make sure that your clients are aware of the full capabilities of your adjusting service. Use every opportunity — over lunch, at seminars, round-table discussions — to advise them of your entire range and spectrum of services. If, for example, your adjusting firm assists clients in fashioning structured settlements, or has a rehabilitation service to return people to work, tell your clients about these services as soon as possible.

Keep clients informed about your company's other cases, omitting names to preserve confidentiality. Clients often enjoy hearing relevant success stories about other clients and the roles played by your claims staff and other staff members representing them.

Keep clients informed about yourself, your firm, your successes and activities. Keep your name and your firm's name in front of the client.

Dear Diary

Do you deliver the claim service that you promise your clients — when you promise it? If not, take another look at your diary system for scheduling work to ensure that you will fulfill your promises.

A tickler or diary system helps ensure that claims work will be completed on time. You can establish a manual system or a computer-based calendar system. Sketch out what you have to do each day, and review your outline before the start of each work day. A good time to plan the next day is the evening before. Weekly planning meetings with your staff to cover priorities — preferably on Monday mornings or Friday afternoons — also will help.

Make sure you keep your files on some sort of regular review, diary or tickler system. This should guarantee that each claim file is reviewed, in general, once a month. There are exceptions, and we will get to those in just a moment. Getting into the habit of using a diary system is an internal office safety system. Consider it quality control for any well-managed claim department. While no system is totally goof-proof, by using a diary system, there should be zero instances of clients writing you or phoning, asking, "Please advise the status of ..." This is a trouble sign.

Unless you opt for some computer software diary system, you will need some type of desk diary or calendar. Nowadays there are dozens of choices. Office supply stores should carry a wide selection. Make sure that the diary you use contains time slots for each day as well as ample room for listing specific files as well as appointments and a daily "to do" list. There are now even software desk calendars and personal organizers which can function as electronic nags to prevent adjuster procrastination.

When you are finished with a particular claim file, page ahead on your calendar and make a note for the date on which you plan to follow up. Then send the file back on its way, place it in your Out box or file it in your cabinet to be pulled later. The file is now "on diary." Using this technique, you should be able to tell which claim files are coming up for review or action in the near future. Some people call this a "tickler" system, a curious but descriptive term.

Using a diary system is an essential quality control step of any well-managed claims office or operation.

Trial dates and other key must-not-miss dates may merit a backup tickler system. For example, in our company, every trial date is logged in the day we become aware of it. The claims examiners must write the trial date, in red ink, on their appointment calendars. In addition, the examiner's secretary logs the trial date on a separate registry. The secretary regularly circulates the trial list, by style of case, trial date, and name of handling claim examiner. This is one way to help prevent slippage and maximize preparation for trials.

Other must-not-miss dates might include:

- Settlement conferences where personal appearance of a carrier representative is required by the court.
- Statutes of limitation on files with promising subrogation potential.
- Deadlines for time-limit demands from claimant attorneys.
- Response due dates for in-suit files for which you have obtained an extension.

Missing just one of these dates can ruin a client's whole day, which in turn, might ruin yours. At worst, it might displease your employer's professional liability insurer. This is another reason why a rigorous diary system, with checks and double-checks, is a prudent risk management step for any claim service. It not only keeps clients happy, it helps keep you out of court ... as a defendant.

There may be some types of claims which are dormant and which do not need monthly review or reporting. Some cases might suffice for an extended diary of 90 to 180 days. If you have placed a file on such an extended diary, let the client know.

Adjusters should adapt the diary interval to the needs of each case. For example, a workers compensation claim involving nothing more than paying a scheduled ppd (permanent partial disability) loss may be able to go 120 days or longer between reviews. A large time-element business interruption lost may merit an adjuster's review weekly, if not daily. The point is that claim professionals should put on their thinking caps so that the diary interval matches the urgency of the case.

While over-diarying is preferable to under-diarying, each adjuster should aim to strike a happy medium. Adjusters will waste their time — one of their most valuable assets — if they over-diary files.

In reporting on claim statuses, adjusters should not hesitate to suggest a diary interval for the client's file. There is no use in spinning wheels on a claim which is inactive and going nowhere. Suggest to the client that the two of you place this type of file on an extended diary, say of 180 days or so. This way, you do not run up adjusting fees for the client in reporting, "Nothing more has happened on this case." It saves the client time that they would otherwise spend in reading a worthless "weather report" which tells then essentially nothing. So now you have saved the client both time and money by intelligent use of your diary system. This pleases clients.

Adjusting offices can use the diary system for other client retention purposes unrelated to file-handling. Make it a point to schedule a trip to visit key clients once a year, for example. Marketing and sales representatives can diary key client birthdays, wedding anniversaries, job or promotion anniversaries, etc. Predate these a week ahead of time to send to clients with an appropriate card, gift or remembrance.

Diaries work. As a claims professional, being diary- and date-conscious is one simple way to keep clients happy. A diary system keeps you moving forward, advancing the ball. On the top of your calendar page for tomorrow's diary, write,

"Start a diary system."

Write Right

Adjusting companies and claim departments should report to their constituencies in clear English, as free of jargon as possible. Most of your clients did not attend law school, are not attorneys and do not read Latin. Therefore, try as much as possible to avoid jargon. Give your clients plain English, not tortured legal prose. Some commentators lament the decline in legal writing skills.

The Texas Bar Association, for instance, sponsors a contests for the worst legal writing (*Wall Street Journal*, 6/26/91). In 1991, the winning authors wrote, "Parens patiae cannot be ad fundadum jurisdictionem. The zoning question is res inter alios acta."

English translation: "The court has no jurisdiction."

A law review article won an award in its category with this entry:

Do the frequent instances today of the lawyer and director bespeak brazenness? Toward clarification and exactitude, a precise review is in order.

Say what?

The Serpentine Monster Award went to a brief submitted to the Texas Supreme Court, a 174-word monster beginning, "So the general rule may be safely stated to be that where there is a general plan or scheme adopted by an owner of a tract, for the development and …" I think you get the picture.

Although these examples are drawn from law firms, adjusters and adjusting companies should heed the message: Write right, in plain, understandable English. Write for the business audience, but do not muddy up your writing with legalese, jargon or Latin; you will impress few and probably lose much of your audience.

Brevity Pays

Be brief. From reading reports or being tied up on the telephone, some clients might think that adjusters believe they are paid by the word. Some adjusters will not use three words when thirty will do. Like adjusters, clients are busy people. Consuming time with meandering blather is a turn-off.

On the phone or in a letter, get to the point. Answer the client's question. Don't dance around it. Claim professionals who are brief show an appreciation for the client's own time demands. Unfortunately, adjusters sometimes forget that clients are busy too. Brevity is not only the soul of wit, but also a welcome trait to the client in any adjuster. The French philosopher Voltaire wrote once, apologizing for the length of a letter, "I am sorry for the length of this letter. It would have been shorter, but I didn't have the time." Brevity does take a little extra planning, thought and effort on the adjuster's part.

Part of being brief involves avoiding insurance jargon and legal-ese. Unfortunately, adjusters and claim professionals are tempted to borrow ponderous jargon and figures of speech from their lawyer counterparts. Perhaps adjusters feel that this lends their communication more weight and authority. Perhaps this reflects their latent desire to be treated on an equal par with attorneys, with whom adjusters often have an inferiority complex. For whatever reason, brevity will be a casualty if adjusters use legal jargon. Screening it out of written correspondence will help claim professionals be brief and get to the point.

Example: Explaining one key policy provision of a liability insurance contract, an adjuster writes, "Under a claims-made policy, the claim must be reported to the insurer *prior to* sixty days after policy expiration."

Solution: "Under a claims-made policy, the insured must report a claim within sixty days after the policy expires."

Comment: "Prior to" is a common and needlessly used adjuster's phrase. It is clunky and almost always a matter of habit which can be unlearned. Use the shorter and simpler word, "before." With the phrase "subsequent to," try using "after."

Example: "Pursuant to my letter to you of 5/3/92 ..."
"Pursuant to our telephone discussion of ..."

Solution: "As I wrote on 5/3/92 ..."
"As we discussed by phone on ..."

Comment: "Pursuant to" and "Per our discussion" are overworked quasi-legal jargon, borrowed from lawyers. It sounds pompous and is verbose.

Example: "Enclosed please find attached herewith our third status report..."

Solution: "Here is our third report ..." Or simply put a caption at the top of the page reading, "THIRD REPORT."

Example: "The claimant advised that she was travelling forty five miles per hour."

Solution: "The claimant stated she was travelling forty-five miles per hour."

Example: "Assuming arguendo that the fire did start with incendiary origins ..."

Solution: "Assuming for the sake of argument that the fire was set by someone ..."

Comment: *Arguendo* is a pompous Latin term meaning "for the sake of argument." For once, sacrifice brevity a tiny bit, use a few extra words and say that.

Example: "During *the course of* our telephone conversation …"

Preferred: "During our phone conversation …"

Comment: Every conversation, by definition, has a course.

Problem: "When the backhoe became engaged as a result of the jump start, it rolled over the decedent, causing his death."

Comment: Between being started and killing the decedent, the backhoe necessarily was engaged. And why not use the person's name?

Solution: "After the backhoe was jump-started, it rolled over and killed Mr. Lopez."

> *Gentlemen:*
> *In re yours of the 5th inst. your hand and in reply,*
> *I wish to state that the judiciary expenditures of*
> *this year, i.e. has not exceeded the fiscal year —*
> *brackets — this procedure is problematic and with*
> *nullification will give us a subsidiary indictment*
> *and priority. Quotes, unquotes and quotes. Hoping this finds you, I beg to remain as of June 9th,*
> *Cordially, respectfully regards.*
> —Groucho Marx, 1928

Brevity in writing and in speech also pays dividends for the adjuster. It saves time which would otherwise be consumed in excess verbiage. Parsimony in speech and in writing frees up time which the adjuster can use for other purposes. Thus, from a time-management standpoint, brevity is an intelligent habit to cultivate.

There is an apocryphal story about the Washington D.C. lawyer Clark Clifford. A client had phoned for advice on a business problem. Clifford listened for a while, saying nothing for long stretches, and then counselled the client by saying, "Do nothing." He thereupon billed the client for $50,000. The client later phoned back, irate, asking why he should pay such a bill. Clifford, according to the legend, replied, "Because I said so," and hung up AND billed the client an extra $25,000.

Forget about the billing part of the fable and the imperious attitude. Remember the brevity part. Get to the point and be brief. Your clients will love you for it.

Toward Better
Client Meetings

Whenever you are scheduled to have a meeting with the client, make sure you are well prepared. Find out who will be at the meeting from the client company and find out what will be discussed. If possible, prepare a written agenda if the meeting is to be anything other than a social visit. Learn in advance what the meeting is supposed to accomplish and what role you might be expected to play in achieving those objectives. Do all the preparation needed to run a successful meeting.

Very often meetings are called only when there are account problems. Rarely do clients seek meetings as mere social calls. Attempt to discern the purpose and agenda of the meeting in advance. Try to pick up signals as to whether a meeting is to discuss account problems. If so, be prepared. Do your homework well in advance, review the claim files or have a digest/summary available. Take a look at recent loss runs, and have them (with extra copies) ready for reference at the meeting. Talk with the key account people — adjusters, supervisors, etc. — who have front-line responsibility for handling the client's cases.

If you know for sure that existing account problems are the reason for the meeting, be ready. Prepare a written "action plan" in advance to present to the client. Anticipate complaints and be pro-active in fashioning the response. The mere gesture of formulating an action plan by itself should at least impress the client that you take its concerns seriously.

This is not to suggest that such an action plan is worthy only for its symbolic value. Quite the contrary. You must back up the action plan with … ACTION. And follow-up. You must be prepared to "close the loop" and get back to the client periodically about progress in correcting problems. You must monitor the action plan for tangible results. If the client ends up thinking that your action plan was an insincere snow job, you have lost credibility, and maybe the account as well. Like virginity, your credibility with a client, once lost, can never be regained.

If the meeting is to be held in your office, have claim files pulled and readily accessible. Make sure that, if at all possible, the other adjusters handling that client's files are in the office and available for any questions or even for introductions. If any audio-visual equipment is needed, have it ready and checked-out in advance. Reserve a needed conference room well ahead of time. Phone the client in advance to see if any special equipment or materials will be needed.

Make the client feel important. In general, do not allow interruptions during meetings with clients. Distractions can upset clients and disturb your ability to concentrate on their claim problems. Focus only on the client and the client's claim when you meet in your office. Accept only "urgent" telephone calls at that time. Instruct your secretary or support staff in advance. Do not hesitate to explain to the client that you have instructed your staff that the only telephone call you will accept during their conference is an "urgent" call.

Make sure you allow enough time to meet with the client. If you have any doubts about how much time the meeting will take, err on the conservative side. If you can, avoid scheduling other appointments and meetings after the conference with the client. Of course, if you know for certain that the client has a time constraint, that is a different matter. You do not want to be antsy, anxious or fidgety thinking about your next appointment as the client is discussing his or her claim problems.

If your adjusting office has a welcome board, make sure the client's names are placed on it in advance. Alert the receptionist to lay out the welcome mat and lay on the big smile.

If you sense a problem, try to be the first one to offer to meet. If you wait until the client thinks it is necessary, the situation may either be out of hand by then or be much less manageable. When you antennae pick up any signs of client unrest, be proactive. If your claims office has a substantial volume of assignments from a client, consider suggesting periodic and regular meetings, whether monthly, quarterly or bi-annually. Such a system of regularly scheduled meetings fosters client-vendor communication, and addresses management issues which staff adjusters, on a case-by-case basis, are ill-equipped to handle.

Always try to schedule client meetings where it's convenient for the client. Be sure to visit their offices more than they come to yours unless, of course, the client prefers it that way. It's always smarter for you to be seen at the client's office by client peers. Carry your firm's banner to the client's shores as often as you can, without being intrusive.

Presenting Your Product

An adjuster's or adjusting firm's services cannot talk! Therefore, try to avoid sending descriptions of them, especially if you are submitting them for the first time around, to the client by mail or messenger. Many adjusting companies have produced slick, multicolored marketing brochures about their businesses. Perhaps a few enterprising outfits have put together their own marketing videos, slightly more effective in these visually-oriented times. These cost thousands of dollars, have lots of visual sizzle but, realistically, a great brochure or video — by itself — is unlikely to land you clients.

High-tech claim operations must also be "high touch." There is often no substitute for the personal touch. Letting your adjusting service's fate ride largely on printed material — no matter how well done — is an invitation to failure. Consigning the pitch to writing only is a sure and simple way to have a plan, proposal or recommendation shot down, deep-sixed or filed away to oblivion. Most clients are inundated with incoming mail and paper. They are awash in promotional pieces from a variety of companies, each promoting its own goods and services. Your slick brochure is not likely to get top priority. As a matter of fact, the client or prospect may consider it intrusive, one step above "junk mail" and toss it in the proverbial circular file. None of us wants to hear this, but it is a common reaction on the part of clients.

Therefore, be sure that you and the key people from your adjusting firm try to meet with the client or prospect *in person* to present, demonstrate and sell yourselves. Be sure that you and your key staff rehearse and practice carefully on how to make the best presentation. In my experience, this preparation is often lacking, perhaps because adjusters pride themselves on being quick on their feet. This is no time to "wing it," although you do not want to come across as an R2D2 robot, either. Perhaps because there is no billing code for "preparing presentation for client," that duty is given low priority. Approach the client presentation with the same thoroughness you would bring to a major claim investigation or project. Wear your best suit. Leave your string tie in the closet at home. Shine your shoes. Polish your presentation. You are on center stage! Leave as little to chance as possible. As one sage remarked, "The harder I work and prepare, the luckier I get."

Be careful about small details as well. For example, make it a practice of sending out follow-up thank-you letters to all the potential clients who attend the solicitation meetings or who give you their time. In some cases, I have seen claim service firms send out these letters via Federal Express so that the recipient receives the communication within 24 hours.

I have been involved in numerous projects involving solicitation of proposals for adjusting services, sometimes on a nationwide basis. Most responses to the RFP's are very impressive. I have always been struck by a number things, however:

1. **Some proposals arrive late.** This is a bad sign. We intentionally put adjusting firms on a 30-day response deadline. We do this even if the placement of an account is not urgent. We do not do this just to yank the chains of an adjusting service though. We want to know how they handle deadlines; can they turn around an assignment? If they cannot get a little thing like a proposal

deadline right, how detail-oriented will they be in handling your claims across the country?

> *Quinley's Corollary 317: Be scrupulously prompt on client deadlines, or request an "extension" with an explanation.*

2. **Some adjusting firms do not respond at all.** This too leaves a bad impression.

> *Quinley's Corollary 65: If you've been asked to submit a proposal but are uninterested, at least thank the client for thinking of you and diplomatically bow out of the running.*

After sending the written material, offer to follow up with a brief verbal presentation. Do this without being pushy. Get your proposal out in front of the client. Figure out some way to make it distinctive.

Periodically review your promotional literature. Is it current? Does it reflect your present staffing and areas of claims expertise? Is it tired and dated? If so, freshen it up!

Listening

In the Woody Allen movie "Take the Money and Run," the protagonist is a ne'er-do-well criminal named Virgil Starkwell, who can't seem to do anything right. Starkwell at one point is caught trying to escape from a prison camp. His punishment: being locked in a room for one hour … with an insurance man! Listening to an insurance person may not exactly be cruel and unusual punishment, but it is not what most clients pay for. Clients pay adjusting firms to listen to them and to solve problems. This does not mean that the adjuster had now become a therapist or psychologist. It does mean that service companies should sometimes ask open-ended questions of the client and then shut up.

God gave us one mouth and two ears and, some have said, we should use them in just that proportion. Yet, listening may not necessarily be a claim professional's strong suit. Claims people tend to be take-charge types. Some of them may feel that talking is a sign of strength to clients and that silence is a weakness. Many marketing types may be so busy giving their pitch that the client often has a hard time getting a word in edge-wise. Sometimes the wisest course is to simply shut up, ask the client open-ended questions, let him talk, and listen closely to the answers.

Jonathan Whitcup is a principal with Consultative Resources

Corp., of Darien, Connecticut. He believes one way to sabotage client relations is to talk too much. This, he feels, is spawned by the attitude — conscious or subconscious, that "I'm much smarter than the customer, who doesn't really know what he needs." (*Success*, May 1992, "Five Ways to Sabotage Your Sales," p. 20).

Adjusting companies will discover, through listening, that different clients have different needs. Ray Waters, national casualty manager for GAB Business Services in Parsippany, New Jersey, explains it this way:

> *"Client needs vary. Some are concerned about promptness, others are more concerned about data accuracy and factors that have little to do with claim adjuster technical skill. Risk managers as a whole are more sophisticated these days, and more and more clients are interested in provider's data capabilities, computer systems, whether your tape drive system is compatible with theirs, etc. Data integrity may be more important to some clients than adjuster qualifications."*

The adjuster or claims professional who listens to the client, and who can listen as well as talk, is worth her weight in gold. Northwestern National, a life insurer, has built its reputation on being the "quiet company," one that listens. The simple act of listening will set you apart from your competition. To be sure, clients go to adjusters for solutions to problems. They expect adjusters to be articulate, assertive and voluble. They do not want adjusters who are timid and taciturn.

However, some clients feel that adjusters simply don't know when to say "when." Ask an adjuster what time it is, and the client is liable to get a lecture on watch history and repair. Lesson: Get to the point. Show an interest in the client's business. Listen to the response.

Part of listening means paying attention to a client's specific instructions. Failure to follow instructions can be a major client sore point, according to Gail Roppo, Atlanta-based Crawford & Company's assistant vice president of market research. "If clients say, 'Take just one photo,'" says Roppo, "just take one photo, not three or four." Pay attention to client instructions, whether they are written or verbal. This is part and parcel of careful listening.

Former New York City Mayor Ed Koch had a habit, during his time in office, of turning to the press and constituents and asking, "How'm I doin'?" Eventually, they told Koch, "Not too good." Still, it was his trademark. Claim professionals should be willing to pose the same question periodically to their insurance clients. This is a way to take the temperature of client satisfaction. They may not always like what they hear, but otherwise they risk living in a fantasy land. They may feel that client relations are just fine when the client holds markedly different views.

A few years ago United Airlines had a TV commercial involving a company who had just been fired by a major client. With rolled up shirtsleeves and sad face, the boss started handing out airline tickets. Management divided up its client list, and sent everyone out to "press the flesh" with clients, before they too became former clients. Of course, all the tickets were on United Airlines, but the commercial's fundamental point was: stay close to your customers. Ask them how you are doing. There are lots of creative ways to gauge this. Suggestions:

- Sending customer satisfaction surveys out on each claim shortly after it is closed.
- Doing random phone surveys of clients.
- Dividing your client list among your staff for contact. Each day, clients are phoned and asked a short list of scripted questions, aimed at eliciting responses about customer satisfaction with the adjusting service.
- Visiting clients and asking them, "How can we serve you better?"
- Bringing clients in to your office, and asking them the same question.

43

- Organizing focus groups of clients, to discuss strengths and weakness of your claim service.
- Conducting "exit interviews" with departing and former clients. Ask them why they left and what could have been done to avert the departure.

Crawford & Company's Gail Roppo emphasizes:

You need to have face-to-face meetings with the customer — by both sales and operations personnel. Use surveys and user groups. Get a group of customers together to discuss needs, what's important to them, what's not, how we can meet those needs, what technology changes are needed, etc.

These are just a few ideas. A creative adjusting service or claim operation can probably come up with some more. They do not cost a lot of money. They are likely much less expensive than having a management consultant come in and analyze your operation.

Listen carefully when clients comment on your adjusting service. Take careful notes to show that you are interested in what they say and have an exact record of it. By following this routine, you should have no trouble establishing rapport and obtaining vital feedback that you can use to strengthen relationships with future clients. Others within the claims department or service should keep you advised in writing of their contacts with clients as well.

In my years of working with adjusting services, I have never had one phone me and ask, "How'm I doin'?" If it happened, I would probably fall out of my chair, for the gesture is so singularly rare. More adjusters should try this.

It takes just a few minutes.

It takes no money.

It takes guts. It takes a willingness to put yourself out on the line. It takes the courage to open yourself up to criticism. No one enjoys criticism. Adjusting services tend to think that if they are not hearing any complaints, the client must be a happy customer. Most adjusters are so busy working cases, that they simply feel they do not have the time to do customer satisfaction research.

Some adjusters get so technically proficient that they eventually grow to see clients as unschooled idiots who don't know what they are talking about. Or, they get so busy moving cases through the system that they don't have time to listen. Or there is no billing code on the time sheet for "Diplomacy" or "Listening to Client." Claims office management is likely so embroiled in the day-to-day tasks of running a busy operation that taking the temperature of client satisfaction seems to be as distant as retiring to Cancun. If customers, policyholders and clients are not calling the home office, the claims manager, state insurance department or writing complaint letters, then everything is probably just fine. Right?

Wrong!

No news is not always good news. There may be festering issues troubling the client of which you are unaware.

Sometimes, though, giving the client what they want is a simple matter. Just ask. You will have plenty of time to talk later. Give your vocal chords a rest. Ask the client questions — in a non-confrontational way — related to your firm's claim service.

Listen to the answers. Distill from them what the client wants.

Then, give it to the client, just the way they want it.

Developing a Newsletter

I get an increasing amount of newsletters from law firms. They seem to be popular with firms, who feel a newsletter is a good marketing tool. It can be an effective tool, or it can be a quick item for the proverbial circular file. I throw most away. Sometimes I have to wonder what constituency and readership the firm had in mind when they wrote the thing. Many of the articles and short "bullet points" are on finer points of law which would primarily interest other lawyers, but not necessarily the client.

This may come as a shock to many lawyers and firms, but most field adjusters carrying a caseload of 275 files could care less what the Third Circuit Court of Appeals has said about the right of "zone of danger" to sue, or the doctrine of Federal preemption.

That is not to say that clients or business professionals are uninterested in the law. However, they need to know what the law is in their particular area OR to know *specifically* how it relates to their claims-handling. Too often, straight reportage of key appellate decisions is of little practical use to clients.

What does this have to do with adjusting services? Very simply, adjusting firms should learn from lawyers' newsletter mistakes and set themselves apart from the competition by publishing a first-class newsletter to clients. Some common errors which lawyer newsletters make, and which adjuster newsletters should avoid:

- Simply reporting a case or claim and its results.
- Drawing no conclusions or those so equivocal that they have no practical use for insurance claims professionals. It's like the lawyer's refrain, "It depends ..." in response to the client's question, "What do I do when ..."
- Failing to explain, in readable English, WHAT THIS MEANS TO THE CLIENT.

These "lessons" from court cases and claims may be self-evident to lawyers and adjusters, but not so obvious to the harried client.

Again, adjusting services should heed the mistakes of many law firm newsletters. Most law firm newsletters to clients are written, not for the clients, but as if they were for other lawyers. The problems are:

- The articles are too technical to be of immediate grasp, import and interest to "lay" (i.e., non-lawyer) readers.
- They are too heavily laden with legal case citations, which the average client will never research.
- Newsletter articles are written in dull "legal-ese" prose.
- There is no practical "how-to" focus on tips which might help adjusters do their jobs better or easier.

There are exceptions. The most effective law firm newsletter I have seen is from the Chicago firm of Conklin & Nybo.

Here are nine tips on how to improve your adjusting company's newsletters to clients:

1. **Report the law:** key case decisions, statute changes, etc. Explain in "lay" terms what this means to the client in the handling of his or her case.

2. **Go easy on the case citations.** Very few business people are going to conduct legal research. For one thing, they don't have the time. If they need the citation to a decision, they can follow

up. Do not write as if you were preparing a Supreme Court brief.

3. **Write in lay terms.** While clients referring claims will typically have a working knowledge of tort law, they typically lack law degrees. Remember, you are not writing for other adjusters or lawyers!

4. **Provide a practical "How-to" focus in your newsletters.** This is really what busy clients are seeking. This alone will make your newsletter stand out among all the others hitting the client's "in" box.

5. **Highlight your victories:**
- Claims abandoned because of your adjuster's investigation.
- Trials won because of the field investigation prepared by your staff.
- Successful motions for summary judgment.
- Voluntary dismissals won.

6. **Profile one of your adjusters** heavily involved in a particular specialty, whether it's surety bonding, ocean marine or jewelers block losses.

7. **Query your readers for their feedback on your newsletter.** What articles would they like to see? Would they be willing to contribute a piece? How informative and useful do they rate your newsletter?

8. **Tie in your newsletter with seminars for clients.** Promote educational forums that you host for clients. For clients who could not attend, report on the educational seminars that you host.

9. **Include useful information** in your newsletter, the type which clients could use. What do clients want to see in newsletters but rarely do? Consider including the following:
- Information about fees.
- Areas of specialization in adjusting service.
- Specialized personnel within the adjusting firm.
- Information about an adjusting firm's particular strengths and weaknesses.

- Material differentiating your firm from your competition.

With a little effort, an adjusting service can give its client newsletter a tune-up and greatly enhance its function as an effective marketing tool for existing and prospective clients.

The Newsletter's
Eight Commandments

If you as a claim service are going to publish a client newsletter, there are certain "commandments" which will help ensure its (and your) success. These are:

1. **Know what your goal is.** Your newsletter should inform AND inspire your clients to do something. Maybe it will get them to lobby about tort reform. Maybe it will prompt them to learn more about your claim service. Perhaps it will contain a kernel of risk management wisdom.

2. **Take a hard look at your newsletter format.** Does it work? Some consultants believe, for example, that newsletters be constructed formally, like a newspaper or magazine, with regular topics — preferably claims-related, covered and revisited regularly.

3. **Choose a realistic schedule.** How often do you want to publish? You are in the claims-service, not publishing business. Do not bite off more than you can chew. Consider starting small, with maybe a twice a year or quarterly publication instead of locking yourself into a monthly schedule. Each claim service company should gauge its needs by assessing when information is needed by clients and what type of information they can use. A workers compensation or group-health oriented TPA will be

heavily focused on job injury and safety issues. An adjusting service which specializes in product liability will gravitate toward issues of design, manufacturing and warnings. Know your audience and use this information in stuffing your newsletter with useful information.

4. **Pick a name for your newsletter which makes a statement.** Be creative if you can, but at least be descriptive. Avoid, for example, naming your publication "Newsletter." Too bland!

5. **Pack the newsletter with news.** Too obvious? Perhaps, but this is advice too often ignored. The newsletter should be a tool which helps build relationships, provide information, educate and advise in a timely manner. The newsletter is a huge opportunity for the adjusting company to communicate information.

6. **Track the newsletter's progress.** Determine when your readers should receive their newsletters, then work backwards from there. Give some thought to printing, copywriting, editing, drafting and even brainstorming sessions for themes and ideas. No job is too small to botch. I recall once when we had to reprint 1,000 newsletters because "Broker Bonus" became "Broker Bonsu."

7. **Give the newsletter spice.** It should not induce narcolepsy, or be a cure for insomnia. Make it interactive. Involve and engage your readers. Have a crossword puzzle, a giveaway, a tearout, a self-diagnostic quiz. Make it fun. You may be pleasantly surprised at the response.

8. **Be generous in your printing plans.** Print more than you actually need. The additional unit cost per copy drops as the printing volume increases. Further, extra copies can be distributed to policyholders, insurance agents and prospective customers.

Telephone Basics

Never have your secretary put a call through to the client and make them wait while you get around to picking up the phone. The message this gives clients is that your time is really much more important than theirs. Even if that happens to be the case, avoid this feather-ruffling phone technique.

Much better is to place your calls yourself. If YOU are placed on hold by the client's secretary, then put it on your speaker phone so you can at least get some work done while you wait. Or, ask the receptionist politely to check back with you in one minute. Or, hang up, call back, and ask to leave a message for a client. Your time is money. Your time is valuable, and there are ways to avoid wasting your time while you are on hold, but do not make the client hold interminably after you have called him or her.

Do not let phone messages pile up. If you cannot return a call immediately, try to return it within 24 hours. If you cannot return the call, communicate with the client through a secretary, assistant or have a co-worker return your call. Be absolutely rigorous in returning phone calls promptly. This is a major irritant to clients. Lack of returned phone calls outstrips billing problems as a reason behind some adjusting firms getting fired. Devise a system for getting back to callers. For example, one strategy is to set aside a block of time each day or to allot time in the evening to return phone calls.

Adopt a "sunset rule" within your claims office. Require that each client's phone call be answered, returned or acknowledged before the sun sets that day. What if you are in the Gulf on a hurricane loss, out of town on another special assignment, on vacation, or in Maui at the latest continuing education offering? Doubtlessly there are times where your ability to address each phone call will be compromised. Plan for this.

Train your staff to handle calls for you as much as possible. They should also be encouraged as well to say, "I'm not sure, let me check on that and get back with you." Make sure to follow through on what your staff tells clients you will do. Rehearse with your assistant or secretary how these situations will be handled. If you are too tied up, ask your secretary or assistant to phone the client that you will be back in touch with them within X amount of time, but did not want the client to think you had forgotten about their call. Clients will appreciate this.

How many times does your phone ring before your receptionist picks up? First impressions are vital, and you only get one chance to make one. You are not likely to lose a client because your phone rings eight times before someone picks up, but it gives a bad impression to your clients. From time to time, pretend you are a client and phone into your own office. How many rings does it take before someone picks up? If it annoys you, just think how it affects your clients. Look closely at staffing and phone lines to make sure that you are not unwittingly giving the impression of a slow, sleepy firm. In today's instant gratification age, like it or not, little things like this will make your firm more user-friendly as a claims office.

Fax Facts

The fax machine is a mixed blessing. Make it your ally. Using it wisely can make clients happy. Otherwise it can annoy and drive clients nuts. First of all, make sure that your office has fax capability. Just having a fax machine can save clients money that would otherwise go toward more costly overnight deliveries. If you can demonstrate to clients that you can (and will) pass the savings on to them, having a fax can please clients. Do not, however, rely on faxing when regular delivery will do just fine. Further, do not use the fax as a crutch or excuse to leave tasks to the last minute. A fax should not encourage procrastination. Restrict its use to genuinely urgent matters. Unfortunately, some adjusters and servicing firms often act like sending a status report by fax impresses the client or anoints that report with special importance. Both reactions are unlikely.

Here is what often happens. The harried client is in the midst of a meeting, file review or other task. A knock at the door interrupts. The secretary breathlessly announces that you have a fax, and hands you the roll of curly waxy thermal paper.

Like most people, you drop what you had been doing to look at the communique. You figure it must be urgent, or else the adjuster would not have bothered to use the fax. You read on, perplexed. As it turns out, the message is a routine status update. Nothing earth-shattering. Nothing time-sensitive. No need for a decision. Just a regular status report.

Far from being impressed by your industriousness, the client is likely to be annoyed, with good reason:

- You have created one more unneeded interruption in the client's day. This creates an opportunity cost.
- You have tied up the client's fax machine when it could have been receiving genuinely urgent communication.
- The client will probably find the fax charge on the adjuster's next fee bill.

Faxing to clients in the wrong way or with the wrong expectations can defeat your purposes. It can also annoy the hell out of clients. For one thing, fax paper — at least the waxy curly thermal paper — looks and feels cheap. Since it is inexpensive, no client is likely to be impressed and say, "Wow, he sent it by fax!" Fax should be reserved for claim reporting situations that are either emergencies — preferably those not of your own creation — or when you do not need for your correspondence to look its best. Another rule of thumb is, shoot out your report or letter by fax only if there is a "need for speed" or if you are reporting to someone you finished impressing long ago.

Beware of sending lengthy fax reports of over, say, five pages. Otherwise, the receiver or client may resent having their machine tied up for so long, their machine paper used up and many minutes reading what is, after all, a rather disgusting form of paper.

Do not necessarily expect the client or receiver to drop everything and reply. The speed of the reply will depend on the urgency of your letter's or report's content, not the method by which the letter was sent.

Do not count on a reply by fax either. At many budget-conscious clients, spending a few extra dollars to send a low-priority letter is an unacceptable response. Feel free to caption your report, "Not necessary to reply by fax," or whatever other verbiage avoids wasted time on the client's part.

A reminder: if the time urgency was created by the adjuster's service lapse, do not bill the client for the fax or overnight delivery charge. If possible, program your outgoing fax transmissions for evening hours, when long-distance phone rates are lower. This can save you (and clients) money. Of course, do not slow down an urgent communique just to save a few nickels off the phone bill. Review the fax charges that you bill back to clients to make sure they are reasonable. Clients often balk at paying $1 per page; this is akin to nickel and dime add-ons which some services (such as hotels) charge.

Another frequent scenario which drives clients nuts: being cavalier in giving them some lead time within which to make decisions.

Example 1: A fax letter from the adjuster arrives dated 4/30. The adjuster must have a decision regarding settlement authority on a product liability claim. He must know by May 1st. One day! The client reviews the attachments, which show that the adjuster knew of the need since April 22nd. This gives the client a mere 24 hours to respond.

Example 2: A frantic fax arrives from the claims rep: She needs a copy of the insurance policy to respond to interrogatories. She MUST have these by tomorrow morning. The client asks, "How long have you known you needed these?" Answer, "Sixty days."

Use fax, but use it judiciously. Reserve its use for genuinely urgent matters. Faster decisions do not necessarily mean better decisions. In fact, just the opposite might be the case. The prevalence of the fax has undermined the art of mulling things over.

Think of ways that you can use the fax to improve client service. A few ideas:

- A fax acknowledgement form, to go to the client the same day a new case assignment is received in the claim office. This fax form also gives the name and extension of the adjuster handling the file, the file number, initial comments about the case, and the due date for the next report.

- A "FaxStatus" form to update clients on late-breaking developments pertaining to their claim.
- A FaxRequest form when you absolutely positively need a prompt decision regarding settlement, defense, payment of a claim, retention of an outside vendor, etc.

Think of frequently-sent letters and forms that typically have some degree of urgency. Try to "routinize" these so that you will have them ready to fax at a moment's notice. Little touches can help the client. If you need a response, put "REPLY REQUESTED" in bold-face caps along the top of the fax transmission. If the fax is merely to report on a critical claim development, label it "FOR INFORMATION PURPOSES ONLY." This helps the client prioritize the need for a response. This is a thoughtful gesture which shows that you have an appreciation for the time demands on the client. Clients have businesses to run. They are busy too!

With fax, though, be selective. Sometimes less is more. If you over-use it, the client may tell you to ... "FAX OFF!"

Client Contact:
Don't Overdo It

Don't overdo contact; be judicious with time demands. This advice might seem paradoxical in light of the messages preceding it. However laudable regular contact can be, there can also be too much of a good thing. Regular contact is good, but a smothering fawning is unwise. If familiarity does not breed contempt, it might generate resentment. Clients are busy. Typically, your client, for example, may shoulder a caseload many times higher than the average adjuster. You see but a small slice of the client's overall caseload and job responsibilities.

If you call, write or visit, make sure you have something to say. Otherwise, don't impose on the client's time. This is, admittedly, a fine line to walk.

If you visit, try not to take up the client's entire day, unless, that is, the client has made clear that she wants the entire day with you. In meetings, as in speeches, you are never going to make enemies by finishing early.

Do not visit when a phone call or letter will do. If you do visit, make sure it is not an impromptu drop-in. Once I was solicited by a marketing representative from a Midwest independent adjusting firm. He just happened to be in the area and though he'd drop in. This shows very little appreciation for the client's time or schedule. Moral: Line up and confirm your appointment in advance. By doing so, you are showing appreciation for the client's time. As a side bonus, you avoid wasting your time by showing up to meet people who are out of the office, too busy to meet, on vacation or out sick.

Do not call when a letter will do. Clients are besieged by interruptions throughout their work day. Do your small part not to add to this, if you can help it. If you phone a client to update them on some aspect of a claim which is not time-sensitive, you are probably not impressing them. Instead, quite to the contrary, you are probably making yourself a bigger pain in the neck to the client who, after a while, will think twice before assigning another case to you. The only countervailing thought is when you know that a client prefers phone communication. Some clients detest being tied up on the phone and are apt to say to you, "Put it in writing." Others are casual about paper, and prefer to conduct business over the phone. Become a student of your client's communication preferences.

Clients keep a mental list of windbags, and unfortunately, some adjusters may find themselves figuring prominently on these registries. If you phone the client, make sure that the matter is genuinely critical. Once on the phone, get to the point. Adjusters are impatient with meandering conversations. State the aim of your call succinctly. Is it to …

- Update? (If so, be brief!)
- Request a decision? (Be prepared to outline the options and make a recommendation.)
- Seek settlement authority?
- Order a settlement check?

Be clear of the aim before you pick up the receiver. The client will appreciate this. Lay people harbor the impression that most adjusters feel that people outside of claims have nothing better to do than to devote their work hours to the adjuster's requests. Business people are often frustrated by their impression that lawyers feel that only lawyers are busy. Make sure that as a claim service provider, you do not expose yourself to the same charge. Adjusters sometimes lament, "That attorney talks like he feels this is the only file I have to work on!" Admittedly, much of this is steam-letting among stressed-out people. However, there are little ways that you can make the adjuster client's job easier by avoiding being intrusive in your time demands.

This does not contradict the earlier nostrums to get out and see the client. Once that is accomplished, however, most clients do not want or need to be fawned over. Keep regular contact, but do not overdo it and do not make excessive or unreasonable demands on the client's time.

Boy (and Girl) Scout Virtues

In our modern high-tech age, we rediscover that old virtues have enduring value. It is true, but bordering on trite, to say that claim service purveyors must win and keep clients the way Boy and Girl Scouts attain merit badges, *they must earn them*!

One way to earn them is by sticking to some old-fashioned virtues which are back in fashion, and for good reason. Read this section and you can truthfully say, "All the important stuff I ever knew, I learned in adjusting kindergarten"!

Punctuality

Be punctual and on time for all meetings and appointments with the client. Never be late. Slovenliness in this area creates a bad impression. A client is liable to think that, if you're not reliable on the little things, how reliable are you on the big things? It is a little thing which erodes trust. Since so much of what adjusters do is time-sensitive, a cavalier approach to appointments bespeaks bad omens to the client.

With my own clients, I attempt to cultivate an impression of split-second responsiveness. You may not know all the law there is to know in automobile defense or product liability, but an iron-clad reliability for keeping appointments is essential.

Admittedly, the unexpected does occur and there may be situations where you are late due to circumstances beyond the adjuster's control. Airlines will kindly serve up reminders of how your schedule can be totally scrambled. If you think there might be any cause for delay, let the client know of this possibility in advance.

When scheduling morning appointments, consider flying in the evening before. If you book an 8:00 a.m. flight out of LaGuardia, O'Hare or Atlanta's Hartsfield Airport, however, don't be surprised when you encounter delays. You are inviting problems. Leave one less item to chance. By flying in the night before, you may be more rested for the morning meeting. Clients do not like to be kept waiting. For one thing, your time is their money.

Be punctual and on-time. This can create the image and reality of service excellence. Consider this vignette:

> *"The day after Hurricane Hugo hit the South Carolina coast in September 1989, Herman Tomer, then a resident of Hartsville, outside of Charleston, opened his front door to inspect the damage to his home. Standing on the lawn, clipboard in hand and pen ready to go, was his USAA agent, who showed up without being called."*
>
> (*Fortune*, 2/10/92, p. 76, "The Payoff From a Good Reputation")

Now, THAT'S punctuality!

Make punctuality a passion. It will win you the respect of clients, customers and policyholders.

Courtesy

It should go without saying that adjusters should be courteous and kind to the client and departmental assistants. Particularly, adjusters should be nice and never condescending to secretaries and others down in the corporate pecking order. Today's secretary may be tomorrow's boss. That "little person" whom you brushed aside or spoke to sharply may be the client to whom you are reporting five or ten years from now. While it is easy to become hard-boiled from handling claims and taking lots of verbal abuse, don't be crotchety. No one likes a curmudgeon or wants to do business with a grump or a bore.

Claim professionals are in the service business. Moreover, they are constantly "selling" ideas and concepts. Adjusters may be selling the wisdom of settling a claim as opposed to defending one. They may sell the idea of defending a claim to a client who is gun-shy about the legal system. They may have to sell the wisdom of their case-handling or investigative approach to someone who is looking over their shoulders.

Personality factors enter into the ease with which adjusters exercise common courtesy. Hopefully, adjusters who specialize in investigating and negotiating claims are in this business because they like to be with and work with people. Nothing could be farther from the cloister than the claims department. Each adjuster must, in effect, be a "human relations specialist." This is what being this type of claims professional is all about.

Be proud of being an adjuster. If you are not happy about doing claims work, then get into some other type of business. Stay happy, and so will your clients. When you meet a client for the first time, try to warm them up and get to know them. Many claim professionals — full of war stories — tend to try to dominate the conversation. Without going to this extreme, one good way to break the ice is to tell a humorous story, preferably a true one. If it is about yourself, where you are the brunt of the joke, even better.

Business etiquette is a topic which could consume many pages unto itself. Client courtesy includes:

- Saying "I'm sorry" when mistakes are made, and taking steps to correct mistakes.
- Returning all client phone calls promptly, at least within 24 hours if not before the sun sets that day.
- Acknowledging all client letter queries within 24 hours and answering such communication within a reasonable time frame.
- Letting the client enter and exit doors first.
- Picking up the tab for lunch or dinner with the client. If the client insists on picking up the tab, accept graciously and make sure you send a thank-you note. Promise to return the favor to the client the next time.
- Thanking clients for their time, and taking time periodically to put into writing sentiments such as, "Thank you for your business."

Do not poke fun at the client, particularly in front of other people. If you have a good personality, this should come naturally. You may get some chuckles, but the client may get the last laugh. Which would you rather be, a comedian or an *employed* claims professional? If you poke fun behind the client's back, beware. You never know who might be in the audience or through what channels such a story might get back to the client. Be discreet and hold your tongue.

There is a saying, "There are two things in life you cannot choose — your parents and your clients." In effect, the client chooses you. There may be some clients you do not like. There may even be some clients you cannot stand. Unless a client asks you to do something which is illegal or unethical, or unless the client is a deadbeat who does not pay bills, the client is still the client. The client may make demands which the claim staff feels is unreasonable. Grit your teeth and check your temper. Blowing off steam may feel good ... for about thirty seconds. The consequences you may pay in lost business or in damaging a relationship may be irreparable. No matter how ridiculous or unreasonable the demand, keep your cool.

Resist the temptation to "tell the client off." Any service company has the option of firing a client, though it is rarely done. If an adjusting company makes a decision that it does not want to do business with a certain client, that is certainly excusable. Rudeness or boorishness is not, however.

If the client does you a favor, make sure you say (or, better yet, write) "thank you." Common courtesy these days is not so common. A habit of courtesy will not only make clients happy, but will make it somewhat easier to get along with other people — claimants, attorneys, policyholders — whose cooperation you need to do your job.

Accessibility

One thing that clients are buying from you is your time, and accessibility to you. Therefore, do your utmost to make it convenient for clients to reach you. Unfortunately, claims and accidents do not take vacations, holidays or sick days.

"It's eleven o'clock; do you know where your adjuster is?" Be sure your clients know when you will be out of the office for extended periods of time, especially key accounts. If you are going on vacation, on sabbatical, on Army reserve leave or back to the home office for an advanced claims training course, consider telling your clients ahead of time. If you are going to be accessible at all, let clients know how they can reach you. If someone else in your claims office is covering your cases during your absence, let that be known, preferably in advance. Example: at Countrywide Services, a specialty claims adjusting firm based in St. Louis, Missouri, each client has seven-day-a-week, 24-hour-a-day access to his or her account manager in case of an emergency during non-business hours.

Get a chart. If your office does not have an adjuster-out-of-town calendar or information center, have one installed. Hang it up near the switchboard or office exit door so that people can check it easily. Your secretary, support staff and boss ought to know how to reach you in case of an emergency, to answer a question, to smooth over a situation, or calm an anxious client until you get back to the office and can deal with it at greater length.

Leave your schedule and itinerary behind. People within your office ought to know your travel schedule, route and hotel destinations as well. Few things are as annoying to clients as phoning in, only to be told by secretaries that THEY don't know when adjuster so-and-so is coming back. Thus, stay in touch and be accessible, not only to your clients, but your support staff as well. Before leaving the office, leave behind a typed itinerary of your schedule, complete with dates, times, locations and phone numbers. Go one step further and leave the fax numbers of those places you will be that you know are equipped with fax capability. Leave a copy with your secretary, if you are lucky enough to have one. Leave a copy with your assistant, your boss and your spouse or "significant other."

If all of this seems too onerous, if this seems like an extreme, then consider whether the claims business is the right one for you. Adjusters are in the service business. You cannot service clients if clients don't know where you are. Access to you is a large part of what they are purchasing. For selected clients, ingratiate yourself by giving them a directory, card or list of your staff's (and your) home phone numbers. If your firm does not provide one, make it up yourself. A wallet-sized home telephone number card listing phone numbers of every person on a client's account team is a great way to impress clients. By giving one to a client, you are telling them, that you and your claim staff are available to service them 24 hours a day, seven days a week.

That's some service!

Remember your other clients. A crucial caveat: Do not let one client play second fiddle to another. When you're out-of-town working for one client, make sure the others know that the work you are doing for them continues progressing smoothly, uninterrupted by your absence. Adjusters often complain about certain persistent claimants and callers, "He must think his is the only file I'm handling." To an extent, clients feel the same way. It bears repeating: As far as clients are concerned, *they* are your only client and deserve your undivided attention!

Honesty

Another no-no is to lie to a client or shade the truth. Never do this. If you do, the truth will eventually hang you. Avoid dealing in hyperbole. Adjusters are conservative by nature, and rarely make extravagant promises, but sometimes marketing, hype or wishful thinking enter the claim defense process, particularly with regard to case evaluation and defensibility assessments. Therefore ...

Don't shade case evaluations. Most adjusters know that there is rarely such an animal as a sure thing. Do not guarantee victory for a client. Do not succumb to the temptation to shade a claim evaluation, either on liability or damages, in order to please a client. There can be a subtle or not so subtle temptation to do this, particularly for eager beaver claim professionals who are sincerely motivated to make a great impression on a relatively new client. Unfortunately, adjusters are often the weather vanes, taking flak from clients for the ills of the tort or workers compensation system. As relates Ray Waters, national casualty manager for GAB Business Services in Parsippany, New Jersey:

> *"Some clients shoot the messenger and get frustrated over the legal system. They may think that the adjuster didn't do a good job by paying a claim*

when, in truth, the problem is with the tort and workers compensation system. Sometimes we have to tell [clients], "You need to write your Congressman."

Resist the temptation to sugar-coat case evaluations in order to earn psychic brownie points with a client. Better to dampen expectations. Even then, some clients will see you simply as a purveyor of doom and gloom. Until there are sweeping tort reforms, there will likely be a class of clients who vent their spleen against the adjuster due to systemic realities beyond the adjuster's control.

Call 'em like you see 'em. Always call it like you see it. If the client has some problem with defending a claim, say so. If an insured has some real problems with liability, be up-front. If the case is a six-figure case, don't wait until the jury is in the deliberation room to make that fact known. Do not embellish or embroider on the truth. In rare cases this may not win you brownie points with clients, some of whom only want to hear what is pleasing. Wise clients need impartial feedback, not yes-men. If a client wants to fire you because they do not agree with your evaluation of a case, you are probably better off without that type of client. Be sincere and truthful and you will be highly regarded.

Credibility is like virginity: You lose it once, and you can never regain it. I recall once organizing an annual seminar meeting for our defense attorneys nationwide. Following the meeting, I received many congratulatory letters on the quality of the meeting. One was from our (then) top counsel in New York City. A few days later, I received another copy of the same letter, only this time it contained a blind postscript which was clearly not meant for me. The gist of the blind P.S. was, "Contrary to my remarks to Kevin Quinley, the seminar was not well-run." He proceeded to criticize many aspects of the meeting.

Although some of criticisms were valid, what was surprising was the attorney's total lack of candor. Had he given me constructive criticism on how to improve the seminar, I would have been appreciative. Instead, he praised the meeting to my face and flogged it to his fellow attorneys. Secretarial oversight resulted in me receiving the errant message. I had to wonder, "what ELSE is the attorney not telling me?" The attorney was suitably embarrassed and made a personal visit to our office to patch things up, but I still could not bring myself to have the same level of confidence in him as I possessed before. Moral: Tell the truth.

Consider biting your tongue.

> **Quinley's Corollary # 143:** *If you can't say something nice about your client, don't say anything at all.*

Be careful what you write.

> **Quinley's Corollary # 144:** *If you do say something scurrilous about a client, be careful where all the photocopies and blind photocopies go.*

Creativity

Creativity is the hallmark of the adjuster and adjusting company in demand. Think of ways that you can creatively serve the client and let them know occasionally that you are thinking of them. One common excuse that clients give for firing a long-time service provider is that the relationship has grown stale. Clients may say, "You're too used to us," or "We need some new blood or fresh thinking." This is why wise adjusters and adjusting companies will strike before the client feels that the honeymoon is over.

Do not take any clients for granted. Strive to do more than what is simply expected of you. Make sure your staff is comprised of self-starters. Come up with new ideas that will help the client. Conventional wisdom was: "If it ain't broke, don't fix it." Unconventional wisdom is, "If it ain't broke, go ahead and improve it." Stir the pot occasionally, even if you think everything is hunky-dory between you and your client. Unfortunately, many adjusters handle claims in a cookie-cutter, routine fashion. The approach is almost assembly-line in nature.

Top-flight adjusters will strive to avoid getting into a rut and will periodically "shake things up" to bring clients fresh ideas. Here are some examples of creativity at work:

1. **Think structured settlements.** Suggest and explore structured settlements. Strive for alternatives to the traditional lump sum payment method of resolving claims. Structured settlements can save clients money. They also provide some tax and financial benefits to claimants. Whereas at one time a claim had to be $100,000 or more to be a structured settlement candidate, that is no longer the case. Now, five-figure settlements are structured. Become an advocate of structured settlements.

2. **Use ADR.** Explore alternative dispute resolution, such as mediation, arbitration, mini-trials, rent-a-judge formats, etc. Do not wait for the client or defense counsel to recommend such measures. The client may not be familiar with them. Defense counsel may be unfamiliar with ADR or may be biased against them, to the extent they cut into legal fees.

3. **Docket monitoring.** Offer a "docket monitor service" for insurers to give advance early warning on policyholders who have been sued in your locale. Or, keep an eye peeled when reading your local newspaper. When it reports on fires, explosions or other high-profile accidents, check to see if your client may be involved.

4. **Educational services.** Offer to conduct in-house seminars on claims for business professionals, do's and don't's of loss reporting, claim prevention, etc. Even if this time is not billed to the client, this time investment will pay dividends.

5. **Start a free newsletter** for your clients, reporting on claim trends, giving tips on loss reporting, case studies (deleting names), and ways clients can help save money, (See chapters on newsletters.) Bonus: this can also be a very effective marketing tool for your adjusting service.

6. **Author white papers.** Author and provide to clients "white papers" on issues pertaining to your mutual business interests, such as disaster planning and recovery, what to do in case of fire, etc.

7. **Use case studies: Learn from your experience.** Publish case studies of claims, omitting proper names in the interest of con-

fidentiality. Extract or distill from each case study certain "lessons" from which clients can draw to improve their own operation. Countrywide Services of St. Louis, Missouri, is an independent adjusting company specializing in product liability losses. In its print advertisements, it is very effective at using case studies, (e.g. "The Case of the Exploding Tire,") to show how they can help defend claims and save money. Consider adapting the concept to your own marketing and communications.

8. **Produce an instructional video** for clients on "How to Investigate Claims," "Anatomy of a Claim," or "How to Team Up With Your Adjuster to Cut Costs." In this visual age, many people will watch a video and use it as a practical training tool for staff.

9. **Produce an instructional audio-tape.** Less expensive than a video is an audio-tape. Some people are just too busy to watch a video, but they will pop an audio-cassette into their car's dashboard during their daily commute. Take the themes that you would put on video and adapt them to an audio format.

Brainstorm with your staff. Every few months or so, shut down the office and unplug the phones. Better yet, get away from the office and brainstorm about new services or enhancements you can offers your clients. Do not evaluate them ... yet. Evaluation can come later. Write down all ideas, no matter how quirky and wacky.

Redefine your business. Are you in the claim adjusting business? Maybe. That is a very narrow way to describe our field. Perhaps you are in the problem-solving business. What loss-related problems do your clients have. Could they use a service which videotapes their valuables and inventory as proof-of-loss in the event of accident? Do they need rehabilitation services? Medical and legal bill auditing? So long as you narrowly define your business mission, you may be overlooking some promising and money-making opportunities. Volunteer to meet the clients needs. Think of what the client's needs are, even if they do not fit neatly within the narrow conventional description of adjusting services. Do not wait to be asked.

Caveat: Be careful not to become too much of an eager-beaver by sticking your nose into sensitive areas where it does not belong. Use your common sense and avoid coming on too strong. Admittedly, this is a fine line.

Think creatively. Generate new ideas. Keep your name in front of the client. There are hundreds of adjusting companies from which clients can choose. Thinking creatively, not falling into the rut of paint-by-the-numbers adjusting services is one way to stand apart from the crowd. You will also find that the job is more fun if you try to break out of a routine mind-set. Creativity enriches your job, making you less of a candidate for burnout.

Loyalty

If you are loyal to clients and deliver good service, they will be loyal to you. Loyalty is reciprocal, a two-way street. In these modern times, jumping from vendor to vendor, playing the game of musical service providers is the norm. Ideally, the adjusting company wants to deliver such terrific service that clients are willing to pay a little extra more. The notion of loyalty to the client sounds almost archaic. What do we mean by "loyalty to clients?" A few suggestions:

1. **Avoid making a claim or pursuing subrogation against the client.** This should go without saying, but it is surprising how often this occurs.

2. **Related to item one, tune up your office's "conflict check" capabilities.** Does your claims office have a way to determine whether any given claim assignment will put you in a conflict of interest with another client? Every claim office ought to have such a system. If not, you are inviting E&O claims against your company. It is a truism in claims as in elsewhere that no one can simultaneously serve two masters.

Aside from the ethical dilemmas posed by conflict of interest, it makes good business sense to avoid conflicts. Assume, for example, that a manufacturer of farm equipment pays your company about $600,000 per year to handle its product liability claims. One of your branches accepted an assignment on a liability claim, on behalf of the dealer/distributor of, say, a tractor. Your local branch places on notice the tractor manufacturer, one of your largest accounts. Tractor Manufacturer will likely not be amused.

If the adjusting company finds itself in a potential conflict situation, there are a number of ways to handle this:

- Immediately alert both clients, and ask them for permission to continue handling both files.
- Assuming client consent, split the handling of the files among separate adjusters or claim examiners. Within some companies, they may go so far as to split the handling of the cases among different people in different branch offices.
- If a client does not wish for you to continue handling both files (an understandable reaction), discern their intentions immediately and honor the client's wishes to have the file sent out quickly to an alternate claim service provider.

3. **Be sensitive to potential conflicts, more of a business than a strictly legal nature.** Do you represent two companies who are fierce competitors in the same field? Coca-Cola and Pepsi, for instance, use separate third party claim administrators. Whether this happened by coincidence or by design is unclear. Some companies might be uneasy about the same adjusting company handling claims for both companies. In a liability claim involving a question of product identification, for example, where would the adjusting company's loyalties lie?

4. **Beware of accepting any public adjuster work, or work from plaintiff law firms.** Some clients might see this as at least a philosophical conflict and turn off the spigot of any new cases. Of course, you might make a business decision that this is a risk that you find tolerable. Perhaps your business volume from public adjusting or plaintiff work contributes positively to your profit and loss. There is nothing wrong with that, as long as you realize the potential to rub your insurance and risk management clients the wrong way.

Be loyal to clients, and they will be loyal to you.

Perseverance

Don't be a nine-to-fiver! This is true, particularly if your clients work long hours. Make sure that they can reach you at your desk during the same period of time they are working.

Again, remember that claim professionals are in the service business. You cannot serve clients if you are inaccessible to them. Although longer hours just for the sake of long hours should not be equated with effectiveness, nobody ever got ahead by just working forty hours a week. Few things impress a client more than when the office phone rings late at night or early in the morning and you pick it up with alacrity. The same goes for the lunch hour.

Nobody — clients included — likes to work or deal with lazy clock-watchers. There is a saying in some offices, "If you don't believe that the dead can come back to life, then you've never been around here at 5:00 quitting time!"

You don't have to go out to lunch each day just because it's there! Consider a working lunch at your desk. If a client is burning midnight oil and working through the day without a lunch break, you can do the same. You can accomplish a lot of good work in the early morning quiet or in a deserted office after closing time. This goes for lunch hours too. You'll get more done and be more accurate with less interruption from the telephone and drop-in guests.

The Care and Feeding of Clients

C lient satisfaction programs do not run on autopilot. Like finely-tuned cars, they need periodic maintenance and tweaking. In the following section you will learn ways to keep clients happy or, in some cases, ways to alienate them. No adjusting text covers this material, but it is extremely important to keeping customers satisfied and happy.

Using an SOP Book

Keep an instruction book on each major client, particularly if they do not have formalized account guidelines themselves. Even for those clients who do have written guidelines — and they are increasingly common — keep a "Standard Operating Procedure" file, folder or book on each one. This can be comprised, for example, of a compendium of procedures peculiar to each client, covering practices which are standard for each particular client, such as:

- billing intervals and procedures.
- reporting guidelines.
- who gives settlement authority.
- who issues settlement checks.

An SOP book can also include "sacred cows" which are idiosyncratic to each specific account. Even clients with written guidelines may not in those guidelines spell out all of their likes, dislikes and "hot buttons." For example, our company loathes a certain type of flimsy, tissue copies which some law firms send. The paper is hard to read, easily susceptible to ripping, and does not hold up well under a yellow high-lighter. We do not spell this out in our litigation guidelines, but often comment upon it to some firms. A minor point, perhaps, but one way that firms can make their communications more user- and client-friendly.

Another claims examiner I know goes nuts when attorneys use evaluation cliches such as "nuisance value," "nominal sum" or "modest amount." He figures he is paying lawyers $100+ an hour to provide more precise advice than this. Only by dealing with this examiner would an attorney learn never to walk into that trap twice.

An SOP book can also be very helpful to each member of your firm, particularly when you or some of your "back up" people are out of town.

Common sense dictates that if the client has written guidelines, you should strive to follow them rigorously. Do NOT assume that these are simply window-dressing, or that every client has a different set, so why read another set. This is a good way to lose business. If you have any questions about the client's guidelines, ask for clarification promptly. If you fail to do so, the client will understandably be unsympathetic when you excuse a breach by saying, "you know, I've never really understood what you were getting at in that part of your guidelines."

Develop written service standards internally, and strive to follow these even if they exceed the client's expectations. Gail Roppo, market researcher at Crawford & Company's corporate headquarters in Atlanta, states, "I don't care whether you're talking about claim service, health care management or risk control services — it is critical to have service standards." She advises that, "The commitment to [service standards] must be from the bottom up and from the top down, throughout the organization." The standards are not something to be paid lip service, observed mostly in the breach or only by the "grunts" working on the front lines.

Making Client
Visits Profitable

Show the flag periodically, especially to your biggest, most important clients. Here are seven suggestions on getting the most "bang for your buck" out of client visits:

1. **Ask to visit the client.** Most clients will be flattered. Unfortunately, too much business is performed by phone, fax and Federal Express. Arranging to visit the insurance client is one way to stand head and shoulders above the crowded competition. To learn about clients, visiting them on their turf pays dividends. As management consultant John Brinkerhoff writes,

> *"Another reason to visit others in their offices is to see that person's environment. People tend to reflect their environment. There is nothing like personal reconnaissance to give you a feel for the values and tribal culture shown by the other person's office. Though offices tend to be similar, an experienced person can tell a lot about an agency and an individual from the layout and decor of his or her office and desktop. So go to the other person's office and learn something."*
> —— "101 Commonsense Rules for the Office"
> Stackpole Books

85

Visiting the client is a tangible and visible sign of your seriousness about the account. It suggests that the client or prospective client is important enough to you and your firm that you are willing to forego some billable hours for business development. Ray Waters, national casualty manager with GAB Business Services in Parsippany, New Jersey, a leading independent claims adjustment firm, explains that, "Adjusting companies must be intensively involved with their clients, doing lots of canvassing, marketing not only current but former clients, staying in touch with formal liaison programs."

2. **Suggest an agenda.** Unfortunately, too many calls from attorneys lack any specific agenda and tend to be meandering chit-chat sessions. This is a waste of the client's time as well as yours. Even if you do not propose an agenda in advance, have one prepared for yourself. Be clear in your own mind: is this a business or social call? Doubtlessly one visit can serve both aims, but the former ought to have priority over the latter.

3. **Provide adequate lead time.** Like attorneys, insurance claims people are very busy. The notion that an attorney can just "drop in" on short notice may be more likely to irritate than impress a client or prospective client. Sure, adjusters' schedules have breathing room ... but not much. Corporate downsizing and trimming of staffs leaves the same work for fewer people. This means that your clients are typically beleaguered by huge caseloads, a reality often grasped by too few adjusters. Therefore, do not call up the client the day before you're going to be in town, suggesting a meeting. Allow more planning and lead time. This sends the message to the client that their time is not as valuable as yours. Save both of you any friction. Give the adjuster adequate lead time for the visit and meeting.

This serves a number of other purposes as well, since it gives you more time to learn about the client and to do your homework.

4. **Be up-front about your purpose.** Do not leave the customer in the dark about why you are visiting. Is it a schmoozing call, or

will you be prepared to review specific files and substantive issues? Prepare your agenda in advance and send it to the client for their input. Allow ample lead time, so that the client does not receive the agenda the day before the meeting.

5. **Be prompt.** Make a good impression. When so much of the claim person's work is time-sensitive, being late is a cardinal no-no. If you are unavoidably delayed due to travel snafus — phone ahead and let the client know. (See section on "Punctuality.")

6. **Do your homework in advance.** Prepare for the meeting. Don't wing it. Have a clear notion in advance of what you want your visit to accomplish.

7. **Invite the client to your office.** Make sure that clients know they are welcome to stop by and visit you. This is simply a hospitable gesture.

Holiday Gifts and Cards

Holidays and other special events offer you an opportunity to solidify your relationship with clients and build up your storehouse of good will. There are do's and don't with regard to holiday cards and remembrances. Attorney and street-smart executive Mark McCormack suggests to business people in his book, "The 110% Solution" that they never SHORTEN their Christmas card list. Adjusting services should ponder this advice.

The point is that once you start this, some people get so used to hearing from you that they will notice it and draw a negative inference if you stop. McCormack's company, International Management Group, regularly sent gourmet popcorn and cookies to clients during the Christmas season. One time he took a client off the list and later saw one of their chief executives, who mentioned that he missed the popcorn.

Some adjusting companies send holiday gifts to clients and others opt not to. Be aware that some insurance companies and corporations, as a matter of policy, do not allow their people to receive "gratuities" from outside service vendors (sorry, but that is the category into which claim service providers are lumped). Consider tactfully exploring this issue if you harbor any doubt. You do not want to inadvertently place your client in an awkward position. It is unlikely that any business is awarded on the basis of a Christmas gift, but it is the perception of possibly being "on the take" that makes some clients wary.

Make your gift something that is not too ostentatious, but which has some practical value for the client. If you can give a gift which ties into your own company's locale, all the better. For instance, my own company has its insurance charter in Vermont. One year we sent our clients and brokers, as a holiday gift, some authentic Vermont maple syrup. Another year, we sent numbered lithographs, suitable for framing, of a snowy Vermont countryside. Some New Orleans defense law firms send "King Cakes" to their select clients during Mardi Gras.

Other years, we have gravitated toward the utilitarian. All of our clients are commercial insurance buyers, with insurance needs beyond just product liability. So, one holiday season we gave each client a book titled, "The Buyer's Guide to the New Insurance Market," published by the John Liner organization. Through special arrangement with the publisher, we had our company name tastefully embossed on the cover. Another holiday season we gave coasters. Yet another, special letter openers. The point is to use some creativity in corporate gift-giving when it comes to clients.

Even if you do not send out holiday gifts to clients, you should regularly update your Christmas or holiday card list. Starting as early as October, start reviewing and culling through your holiday card list. Be sure that it is current. People change jobs as well as titles. Make sure you pay attention to these and get them right. Last year's list may be woefully out of date. Check for correct spelling of names, especially unusual last names. All your effort to remember a client with a card may be in vain if you botch the spelling of a name. I cannot tell you the exact number of cards or letters I have received from law firms and other service providers addressed to Kevin Quinely, Quigley, or Quinlan.

If you are going to go to the trouble of sending out holiday cards, go the extra step and hand-write a brief message inside. This shows some personal attention and thought went into the card. The inscription need be nothing elaborate. It can be "Happy Holidays, Burt!" or "Thanks for your business," or "May you and your company have a prosperous New Year," or "Thanks for all your help on the claims." If you can tailor the card more precisely to the interests of the client, even better.

Rethink your company's holiday card policy to see whether there are better times to send cards so your message does not get drowned out. For example, a few firms send Thanksgiving cards because fewer people send these out and Christmas- holiday cards tend to all blur together, due to the greater volume. A greeting during Thanksgiving may be noticed more than another card which arrives during the flood of Christmas holiday mail.

Do not feel that you are necessarily locked into the conventional mold of only sending cards during the Yuletide holidays. Other occasions may lend themselves to sending cards to clients. Examples:

- St. Patrick's Day.
- When a client renews its coverage or claim service contract with you.
- After a new assignment.
- The client's birthday.
- Client's anniversary date with his/her company.
- Client's promotion or notable achievement; a congratulatory card works fine here.
- Sympathy card for death in the family.
- Congratulatory card upon the birth of a child.
- Get-well card after recent surgery, hospitalization or illness.

(No, I am *not* getting a retainer from the greeting card industry for these ideas.) The point is to think of ways to get your name in front of the client, and to show some thoughtfulness. Clients may remember your thoughtful gesture for many years. Cards cost just a few cents, but their impact can be positive from a business standpoint. This is not to suggest that you do anything with which you feel uncomfortable. Do not send a card if you don't feel right about it.

Job Titles

It should go without saying that you should get your client's job title right on all correspondence. You may not be hung up on job titles, but I suspect it does make a difference to you whether you are referred to as an adjuster examiner, supervisor, manager, etc. for example. Promotions and new titles do not come easily. People may outwardly profess that titles are unimportant. In our egalitarian times, this is fashionable. It may be sincere, or it may be posturing. You are better off erring on the side of caution and treating the job titles of others, especially clients, as important.

Pay attention to your client's stationery, letterhead and business cards. Keep your antennae tuned. Be alert to new job titles, promotions, even demotions within your client's corporate structure. How do you do this?

Read the trade press to see who has been promoted. *Business Insurance*, for example, makes note of industry comings and goings, particularly of risk managers who are big purchasers of adjusting services. (Hint, hint!) *National Underwriter* and *Claims* also have brief coverage of people moving up in the insurance industry. Send a congratulatory note or card. Pay special attention to ensure that your secretary makes the title change in her

Rolodex, word processing memory, etc.

If your office keeps central files — either hard copy or on computer — of client information, make sure you keep a key contact listed, and update that periodically as you become aware of changes within the client organization. The client won't really care if you try to blame your clerical staff for the fact that you are still using the old job title! It will only make you look bad, as well.

In the client world, there is a relative abundance of job titles. Let me put it this way. I am not hung up on job titles, BUT I AM hung up on my client's job title. If you address a letter to a Claims Manager by using her old title of Claims Examiner, she likely will not appreciate it. She may be downright offended. Chances are she worked hard to get that promotion, and feels somewhat slighted by the adjuster who can't get a little thing like this right.

Did I say "little thing"? If it's your title being bungled, it may not be so little. It is another one of those signs telling the client how detail-oriented you are … or aren't. If you can't get the little things right, what confidence does the client have that you will get the big things right? This may not be fair, but it is the way many clients think, consciously or subconsciously.

Pay attention to demotions and lateral moves as well. For an adjusting service, these may spell opportunity or peril. If your chief advocate and tie to a company is demoted or moved aside, that may not bode well. Maybe the new person will have prejudices at odds with your aims, will champion a competing adjusting service, or believe that all adjusters are worthless. Time to plot your mew approach and to intervene. You may have some fast "rehab" work to do to establish a positive relationship with the new person in charge of claims and claim assignments.

Make it a habit to ask for business cards. Keep these for reference. You can buy handy sheets that go into three- or six-ring binders for saving these. The client's business card has his or her job title, usually just the way they like it. Be a (business) card collector.

Pay attention to not only special announcements from clients regarding promotions, etc. Pay attention to the way they sign off on letters. If there is a change in job title, make a careful note of it and instruct your secretary to do the same.

If the client gets your job title wrong, pretend that it did not happen. Think twice about correcting the client. Give them your business card. Between that and the way you sign off on your letters, they should be able to get your job title right. If not, grin and bear it. They can call you anything, unless it's "former adjusting service."

Taking the Blame:
Seven Ways to Admit Mistakes

If you or one of your staff has goofed, go ahead and take the responsibility. No one is perfect and clients do not expect you to be right all of the time. Maybe an adjuster failed to do something that the client specifically requested. Or, the sin might be one of commission where the claims representative did something he or she was not supposed to do. Perhaps the adjuster failed to report, to return phone calls or to answer an inquiry. Maybe the offense was more egregious: an adjuster forgetting to assert a compensation lien, or to refer a file out to counsel for subrogation pursuit before a statute of limitations ran. Whatever the transgression, if you goofed, admit it as soon as you can to the client.

This does not necessarily go both ways, however! If your client has erred and you have documentary evidence that conclusively proves them wrong, tread cautiously. One can be right and still lose. You can be correct, and still lose an account or a client's good will. Remember the old adage that there are two rules of business:

Rule #1: The customer is always right.

Rule #2: When in doubt, refer to rule number 1.

Nobody likes to be reminded that they made a mistake. Adhering to the adage that the customer is always right — within reason — will help ensure that you always have clients.

As soon as you learn that you or someone in your adjusting firm or claims department has made a mistake, be sure to let the client in on it. Don't try to stonewall it or cover it up, hoping it will disappear. Best to face the music immediately. Call, write or visit the client as soon as possible and say, "Mea culpa." In this way, you can both get together and jointly figure out the best possible way to correct the error and to repair the situation. Adopt Harry Truman's adage: "The buck stops here."

Consider the following ways of dealing with poor claim service which your client has noticed:

Apologize. This costs no money, just a little pride. Be sure to say "I'm sorry." Even if deep down you do not think that you or your firm did anything wrong, you can still be sorry that something happened. This way, an apology should not cause your errors and omissions carrier to become apoplectic. Consider the way you phrase your apology as well. To clients, it sounds more sincere than "We're sorry." Swallow your pride. Efface your ego and apologize.

Move fast. Decisiveness counts here. You are driving an ambulance, not a hearse. Acting fast to right a wrong lets clients know you care about what they think. It also allows you to move before the problem or resentment festers.

Show empathy. Clients need to know that you care about them. Moral: Treat the person first, then address the claim problem. A simple "I know how you feel" may do the trick. It cannot be a trick, however. It must be heartfelt.

Atone. In addition to correcting the problem, go a step further. Sometimes the mistake cannot be undone. You cannot turn back the clock. If some service lapse has occurred, deal with it. Offer to waive or reduce charges. Offer a freebie in exchange. Ideally, this works best if you do it before clients express their anger. It shows that you understand the problem and want to correct it.

Follow up. Ask clients if they are satisfied. This shows that you care and offers you feedback on how you have handled the problem.

Don't finger-point. Resist any temptation to lay the problem on your firm, your boss, your subordinate or your secretary. Trying to duck responsibility will only irritate the client even more. It implies lack of accountability in that you are always blaming someone else for your problems. There is another reason to avoid finger-pointing. It is also no way to build morale within your own department or firm — something which is key to delivery of top-notch service.

Learn. If there has been a genuine goof, look at the episode as an opportunity to learn and improve your service. What can you do to prevent a situation like this from recurring? Do you need more staff training? Tighter supervision by mid-level management? Closer file reviews? Iron-clad diary or tickler systems? New procedures? Last but not least — do you have sufficient staff? Many servicing problems are directly traceable to chronic under-staffing in the claims area. Take a hard look at staffing and ask yourself if mistakes are the result of trying to do too much with too little staff. If so, hire and train. The point is that you can turn the negative into a positive if you learn from the mistake and undertake steps to prevent problems from recurring.

Making Recommendations

Do more than simply be a messenger for the client. Examples:
An adjuster reports:

"The claimant wants $5,000. Please advise."

Or, "Claimant's counsel has now given us a $20,000 demand, with a 20-day time limit for a response. Please advise what you would like to do."

Clients pay you, in part, for your advice and recommendations. Give it to them. They are free to heed or discount your recommendations. After all, they are the clients. Give them your recommendations, though. Otherwise, adjusters become mere messenger boys (or girls), performing a job which most anyone could accomplish.

For claim services wishing to break away from the pack and differentiate themselves from their competition, this may be one effective shortcut. Charles Caronia of Caronia Corporation states that, "Out job is to make informed recommendations, to give pro's and con's. You may not agree with our recommendations, but we're going to give them to you." Two heads are better than one and, as a result, Caronia often has more than one claims examiner review a file to pick up something another one missed.

John Nelson, marketing manager for Countrywide Services, a product liability claims firm, states that, "the economy has everyone struggling to get the most from their expense dollar and our ability to make accurate recommendations on how much investigation is needed and whether to settle or try is critical."

> *"Behold the lowly turtle. He only makes progress*
> *when he sticks his neck out."*
>
> —Anonymous

Stick your neck out. Suggest alternatives. Outline options. Make recommendations. Then and only then, request the client's advice. It is the client's call. "At the end of the day," states Charles Caronia, "it's not my claim, but the client's." It's their money. So, do not take it personally if the client does not accept your suggestion or even disagrees with your recommendation.

In example two, above, it would be preferable for the adjuster to report:

> *"Claimant's counsel has demanded $20,000 and*
> *has made a 20-day time limit demand.*
> *As I see it, our options are:*
> *(1) Reject the demand outright, and prepare to*
> *defend the case through trial.*
> *(2) Accept the demand.*
> *(3) Offer a lesser sum, say $10,000, within 20*
> *days.*
> *(4) Attempt to get an extension on the rather*
> *arbitrary 20-day deadline.*
> *(5) Defer a decision until the investigation is*
> *complete.*
> *I recommend option number ____. Please advise*
> *as soon as possible so that I may respond in one*
> *way or the other to claimant's counsel."*

Don't namby-pamby and drop the problem in the client's lap. Make the tough calls, and leave the final decision to the client, unless they give you carte blanche. Decisiveness is a virtue, but try to have all the facts at your disposal when you make a recommendation. Unfortunately, there is probably too much of a "paralysis of analysis" among many claim staffs. Sometimes it seems that no one wants to make a decision, perhaps in fear of being wrong or being second-guessed. There is a constipation of decision-making, a risk-averse atmosphere where no one is willing to step in and make a decision. As a result, delay often ensues, the claim department's image is sullied and, sometimes, the delay gives rise to bad faith claims.

Stick your neck out and make a recommendation. Clients need professional advice and recommendations, not tea and sympathy. Outline for client's the pro's and con's, the advantages and "down-sides" of each course of action.

Friendship

Clients are people too. As long as you have to deal with them on an almost daily basis, it may be a good idea to nurture your business relationship into a long-lasting friendship. Frequently, this happens without you knowing it. It can be extremely rewarding, especially insofar as the longevity of your tenure with a client is concerned.

Examine your own feelings on this issue. Do you insist on keeping your business and social lives separate? Are you afraid that clients or prospective clients will refuse your invitations? Either of these attitudes can be counter-productive to claim professionals or services wishing to develop a sound and growing client base. Clients may decline invitations, but few are offended by them. Take a chance and ask. In tight economic times, clients probably receive fewer and fewer invitations. Those that they do receive may be more appreciated. Hence, while in recessionary times it may be tempting to cut entertainment budgets, a tight economy may be precisely the time to do just the opposite.

To avoid conflicts of interest and breaches of ethics, some clients have strict internal policies banning the acceptance of "gratuities" from outside service providers. Adjusting companies are outside service providers. Some firms might consider social invitations — tickets to ball games, dinners at fine restaurants, invitation to a seminar at a resort location — to be gratuities. If you know for a fact that the client company has such a policy, then tread cautiously. Still, there is nothing wrong with cultivating a friendship with a client.

There are varying schools of thought with regard to making friends out of clients. One school of thought is that you should avoid it. Keep your social and professional life separate, hermetically sealed. Some might call socializing with clients brown-nosing. Whether or not this is true, it can complicate business if service or relationships go sour.

Remember the saying, "Never mix — never worry"? This can hold true with regard to mixing friendship with business. It is one thing if you flub an assignment for a business client. You may never do business again with that client. If you flub it for a friend, there are lots of complications. It is like the old adage never to lend money to a friend, you may lose both. Or, never sell a used car to a friend. That way, if the deal goes sour, you will only lose a customer, not a friend.

By making friends out of clients, however, you may further cement your relationship. You may make the client/friend more impervious to the blandishments of competitors. You may hold on to that client longer. There may be some drawbacks, though. You may be held to a higher standard of performance in your job, even to an unreasonable and unrealistic degree. To avoid charges of favoritism, the client may hold you to an even higher performance standard. If you ultimately have to part company — for any reason — you may end up losing not only a client but also a friend, and leave hard feelings. If you feel this way, there is nothing wrong. If you do not care for your clients, do not try to be someone that you're not by socializing with clients. If you feel hypocritical doing it, don't do it.

The other school of thought is that you develop business contacts by nurturing social relationships with business clients. On the other hand, new business opportunities may open themselves if you (occasionally) mix your personal with professional life. If you do not care for your clients, maybe you should consider looking for another line of work, one where you can choose your own clients, or where you do not have clients. As one sage observed, "There are two things in life you cannot choose: your parents and your clients." Another word for those people without clients is "unemployed."

From the time you graduate from adjuster training school to the time you retire at 65, you will have put in 41 years of crawling and scratching your way up the claims hierarchy. To make your adjusting practice palatable and even have some fun doing it, enjoy the work that you're doing. Go ahead and make friends with business associates and clients, if you're so inclined. You may even like it.

Receptionists

An adjusting company's receptionist can help or hurt its image. While these employees may be the lowest-paid in the firm, if they rub clients the wrong way they can be the most expensive. Abrasive or indifferent receptionists can do damage to a client's relationship that the most articulate status report cannot undo. This applies not just to law firms, but to all service businesses as well.

Receptionists who answer the phone in a bored, hurried or abrasive answer are a definite turn-off to the clients, policyholders and significant others. Make that *any* client.

Call a firm in New York City, and you're likely to hear:

"Lawofficespleasehold"

I swore once that one of my defense firms was named Segal McCambridge and ... Pleasehold.

Pay attention to the "little things" which put visitors and clients at ease in your office. Ask your secretary or receptionist to note and remember what clients enjoy when visiting your office — coffee with sugar, no cream, a Diet Pepsi, access to a telephone, or copies of documents to read. Keep in mind as well communication preferences among clients. Some prefer to communicate in person, others by phone, memo or letter. Follow the client's preference whenever possible.

How about hiring another backup receptionist? Or throwing for another incoming phone line? It is very frustrating and demoralizing to the client to phone the adjuster, and be placed on hold indefinitely by the receptionist. Or, to be placed on hold for five minutes, and then be disconnected, holding a dead line.

Other clients feel that whether the adjuster is in the office or not (read: willing to speak on the phone) depends on who is calling. Example:

Client phones the adjuster. Seven rings.

"Claims department."

"Yes, this is Kevin Quinley. Is Ms. Wright in?"

"May I tell her who's calling?"

[This really does not answer my question. Does the caller's identity determine whether attorney Wright is "in" or "out"? As a client, am I "in" or "out"? Am I important enough to be granted an audience, or will I be cast into the sea of pink message slips?]

"I'm sorry, what did you say your name was?"

"Quinley. It not only was, it still is."

"Please hold."

Receptionist back on line: "I'm sorry, may I take a message?"

"Yes, could you please ask her to file on the *Hughes* case . . ."

"Excuse me, please hold."

You get the picture.

Clients also hate being placed on hold for long stretches of time, or disconnected. No one likes listening to Muzak. Instruct receptionists to check back frequently with callers to let them know at least that they have not been forgotten.

In a perfect world, these types of factors should have no bearing on which adjusters or adjusting firms are favored, and which ones are not. In the real world, however, such factors enter into client decisions. Polite, interested and gracious receptionists can be one intangible which can make your claims department or adjusting firm more user-friendly to your clients or policyholders.

Remember that receptionists are people too. Give them time, recognition and pay them competitively. The position can be tough, tedious and thankless. Take time to thank them for jobs well done, to make their jobs interesting and communicate with them. Receptionists are on the front lines, often taking the verbal abuse and covering for you, keeping irate people at bay under very trying circumstances. Invest time in training them and in making their jobs as tolerable as possible. Remember them during birthdays, job anniversaries and Secretaries' Day. Let them know what is going on within your company, so that they see the big picture. Keep the receptionists happy, and they will more likely than not see to it that they keep your clients happy. That is a fair trade-off!

As I pen these lines, I am on hold, waiting to see if Ms. Wright is in ...

21 Tips for Better Adjuster-Client Relations

Monetary goals and production/billing quotas may easily become guiding principles for independent adjusting services whose attention is focused on the bottom line rather than on client service. Too often, perhaps, accountability to a billing sheet replaces accountability to the client. Clients are often skeptical about dealing with adjusting services. Many have pet horror stories about how some rosy-cheeked adjuster bungled their claim. I attended one lawyer-sponsored seminar where a speaker suggested that most adjusters in their current jobs were pizza delivery-men in a former life. This is the image we have to deal with ... and overcome.

Clients are searching desperately for personalized service from adjusting professionals who are concerned about them, their business, their problems and who are willing to view their claims in the broader business context. They want claim professionals with good reputations who are honest, skilled in the art of listening and who are competent and efficient.

John Nelson, marketing manager of Countrywide Services, cites the following as positive "hot buttons" which impress clients:

- Immediate responses (even on routine items).

- Accessibility (immediate and consistent).
- Achieving results beyond expectations (i.e., hitting the home run).

Try hard to think of your clients as people as well as cases, assignments and claim files. Everyone likes and appreciates attention. Therefore, some Do's and Don't's for better relations with your clients:

1. **Do whatever you can to improve your listening and other communication skills.**

2. **Appreciate the honor of being chosen to serve your clients.** They can easily go down the street, or down the directory, and find someone else to handle their claims.

3. **Do whatever you can to be client-oriented, even if your or your company's adjusting practice is specialized in a particular field of claims.** Ask yourself whether your department or office is customer-driven. Make sure you evaluate each alternative with the consideration: Would this benefit our clients?

4. **Remember that your clients have feelings and are hungry for personal attention.** In your rush to "get the job done," make sure you show an interest in the client beyond a particular claim file.

5. **Do your best to give clients reassurance, encouragement and even inspiration.** Do not paint too rosy a picture for them, though, just to make them feel good. Give them the risks and down-sides. Under-promise and over-deliver.

6. **Do not be aloof or patronizing to your clients.** They may not know the technical side of claims adjusting as well as you do, but they know what they like and what they don't like. If they feel they are being taken for granted, they will "vote with their feet" and move their business elsewhere.

7. **Do not neglect your human-relations skills.** Technical proficiency and an alphabet-soup listing of professional designations cannot replace the human touch.

8. **Do not be indifferent to the need to inform and educate your adjusting clients.** View your job in the broader context of

educating your clients. The more they know, the better the two of you can work together. An educated consumer really is your best client.

9. **Do not think that you are entitled to a successful adjusting practice just because you have your adjuster's license or professional designation.** Designations are nice, but as the saying goes, "People don't care how much you know until they know how much you care."

10. **Do not view the client as a necessary evil, or as a nuisance who gets in the way of you trying to do your job of handling claims.** Without the client, there is no paycheck.

11. **Promptly return all phone calls.** Sometimes it's the little things which drive clients away. In a perfect world, decisions might not be made on this basis but in the real world, they are. Phoning back shows you care and value the client.

12. **Do not simply meet your client's expectations.** Exceed them.

13. **Understand and define your client's objectives.** How does your client approach the claims process: As a chance to:
  • Defend a company's honor?
  • Prove a point?
  • Punish the claimant?
  • Get rid of the case?
  • Save money on legal fees?
  • Squelch a dangerous precedent?
Probe to learn and understand your client's claims philosophy. If they don't have one, help them to shape one. If you don't know what it is, you will have a difficult time serving them the way that they like.

14. **Develop a claim plan for each client, at least on major claim assignments.** Give the client a copy. This should show steps one, two, three, etc. regarding the claims.

15. **Review and make sure the client understands the risks in any procedure or investigation you recommend.** Any alternative — from denial of a claim to payment — has certain risks. Just as

prescribing doctors warn of contra-indications or risks from certain types of surgery, the adjuster must outline potential drawbacks in any claims recommendation.

16. **Reinforce the elements of your adjusting firm's service strategy with an annual retreat for everyone in the company or claim department.** (For more discussion, see the chapter "Hold an Annual Client Service Retreat.")

17. **Reward adjusters and all employees for being client advocates.** Each member of your staff should be encouraged to become champions of the client's interests.

18. **Suggest realistic and commercially acceptable solutions.** Make no "pie-in-the-sky" recommendations.

19. **Give the client enough paper to know what is going on with his or her claim, but do not "shower" the client with needless paper.** Remember the rain forest and save a tree.

20. **Greet each client in the reception area and make sure each feels at home in your office.** Start off on the right foot and do not make clients cool their heels in your waiting area.

21. **Ask questions to determine all your client's needs, not just those in the field where you happen to be handling their claims.**

In every claims office there is a compelling need for adjusting staffs to get organized and take control of their time. With proper organization, efficient administrative and procedural systems and well-trained personnel, we should discover we have more time available. We should use that time to focus in on clients and their needs, and to provide personalized service. One additional benefit: adjusters will derive more personal satisfaction from being in the claims business.

Making Assignments
a Pleasant Experience

Good service is a collection of little moments, contacts which may last just a few minutes apiece but add up to an overall impression. For many adjusting services, the first opportunity to make a good impression is in taking in a new assignment.

Consider giving clients personal files of their claims for their own convenience and record-keeping. Provide clients with a file folder that shows the name of your adjusting firm, address and telephone number. They can use the folder to hold material you give them — brochures on your adjusting service, pamphlets with a step-by-step description of the claim adjusting process, copies of written reports prepared by your claim staff on their behalf, and claim status reports.

By all means, let clients know that you would appreciate handling their claims in other lines. This seems simple enough, but asking for new work is something that many claim professionals either forget about or feel uncomfortable doing. If you handle a workers compensation account, ask about handling the client's general liability claims. If you have the GL, ask about adjusting work on the corporate or fleet auto side. Show a sincere interest in your client's affairs. Learn all you can about their business.

Do not forget to say "thanks" for a new case assignment, particularly if you are an independent adjusting firm which typically receives new assignments one case at a time. Pay attention to the way that your staff is accepting assignments over the phone. In some busy claim offices, taking in new assignments over the phone is a dreaded chore. Make sure that adjusters or others taking in phone assignments realize the importance of being upbeat and appreciative, not preoccupied and distracted. Let a smile show in their voice.

Keeping Current

Few patients would want to go to a doctor who did not keep up with the *New England Journal of Medicine*. Any self-respecting attorney reads the *ABA Journal*. As professionals, adjusters must similarly stay abreast of legal, medical and investigative developments in their field of claims. This includes policy form changes, court decisions affecting investigation or news on what other insurance or adjusting companies are doing to make their operations more efficient. Adjusting is a multi-disciplinary field, drawing from areas of law, medicine, private investigation, human relations and insurance coverage. To service clients effectively and keep them happy, though, claim professionals must keep current within their field.

Sadly, many claim professionals can feel overwhelmed by their workload that they view such reading as a luxury. The challenge of carving out time to stay current is not limited to the claims industry, and it reaches into the confines of the top corporate boardrooms. In one survey of 500 CEO's, 83 percent reported that they lacked time to keep up with reading in their own field.

Still, claim professionals worthy of being called "professionals" must find ways to carve out time to stay abreast of developments within their niche. For example, to be more interesting and informed for your insurance clients, you should read *their* trade publications to keep current and conversant with issues germane to the field. If your assignments come from insurers and risk managers, you should devour weekly issues of the *National Underwriter* and *Business Insurance* at minimum. You should skim every issue of *The Wall Street Journal, Business Week, Fortune* and read the pertinent articles.

If your clientele is more specialized, so should be your reading. Handle lots of workers compensation? Read *Occupational Safety and Health.* If your clients are car companies, you would want to keep on top of the trade press covering the automotive industry. If you service health care providers, read *Hospitals* magazine and *Perspectives in Health Care Risk Management,* published by the Association of Healthcare Risk Managers.

To keep abreast of trends in the adjusting profession, read *Claims* magazine. No other nationwide publication has such broad coverage focused exclusively on the loss adjusting industry.

There are a number of legal publications, such as *For the Defense,* published by the Defense Research Institute, discussing law which bears upon adjusting work.

A few caveats about legal publications, though. First, much of the law they discuss may be in jurisdictions far afield from the one in which you work. The law elsewhere may have no bearing on your state. Second, many of the legal articles are too esoteric to be of much practical value. Law publication articles rarely distill findings into practical tips. If they do, they are likely to revolve around trial tactics and discovery, topics with little day-to-day value to the average adjuster's work. Finally, too many of the legal publications are a recitation of appellate court holdings, with little or no practical advice on how this can be distilled for value to the real-world claims operation.

Time-pressed claim professionals will doubtlessly find it a challenge to stay current with their reading. The mental and physical demands of handling claim files is sufficiently draining as to diminish the energy for reading. Moreover, time is in short supply. A few tips for adjusters on how they can keep current — for their own benefit as well as for their client's:

- Keep a "Reading File" for business travel, lunch breaks, waiting periods or other scraps of "down time." Keep in this file material which deserves your attention, but which does not have to be read immediately. Store the file in your briefcase.

- Develop the art of skimming. Do not sit down and read all the magazines or journals cover-to-cover. Scan the table of contents quickly to see what articles hold your interest. Zero in on those articles and skip the rest.

- Use the "rip and read" technique. Skim periodicals for articles that seem to be interesting. Tear out the article you wish to read, or photocopy it. This also prevents your in-basket from starting to resemble the Leaning Tower of Pisa, and keeps you from becoming the reason for the department's bottleneck.

- Remove yourself from reading lists of periodicals which have no direct application to your cases. Your reading time is limited and must be intelligently rationed. One way to make time for necessary reading is by being selective in what you do read. Get off of mailing lists that hold no interest. Ask that your name be dropped from circulation and distribution lists on periodicals that have no application to your job.

- Consider taking a speed reading course. Many are relatively inexpensive, and some offer free lifetime refresher courses. If you can show a direct payback to your job, consider approaching your employer to see if they will cover all or some of the cost.

If business and insurance is your chosen field of legal specialization, it is vital that you become a good source of information for what is happening in it. Read the leading weekly and monthly trade publications devoted to insurance defense and practice. Read weeklies for news and monthlies for "how-to" tips. For an overview of big picture business trends, become a regular reader of *Fortune* or *Business Week*. Poke your head up out of the adjusting hole and make sure you are attuned to what other businesses — not necessarily the claims or insurance fields — are doing. Broaden your vistas.

Claim professionals do not have to become "grinds" in order to stay current. All it takes is a little discipline and wise budgeting of time. Those adjusters and companies who go the extra mile to stay current will have a competitive edge over their rivals.

Out-of-Town Clients

Occasionally, the adjusting company representative will have a chance to call on the out-of-town client. Adjusters and adjusting company representatives should cultivate such opportunities, within reason.

An important rule when dealing with out-of-town clients is that you can't be in a hurry to fly, drive or take a train home. Do not seem preoccupied with your return travel arrangements. This is insulting to clients and lends the impression that your top priority is to leave them. That does not make for a good impression. When a client asks you about your return travel arrangements or reservations, tell them you are on no special timetable, you'll return home only when the work is done.

If necessary, volunteer to stay another day or so. It is insulting to the adjuster's client to arrive at a their office a 9:00 a.m. and immediately ask the client to have a secretary confirm your travel arrangements for your trip home. Your main job is to service clients. You cannot do this effectively by rushing away to another appointment or returning home early. If you must confirm travel arrangements, be discreet. Do not ask the client's secretary to do it. Ask if you can borrow a phone, preferably in an unused office or conference room where you will have some privacy.

New Staff Announcements

Each week I receive in the mail one or more engraved cards from law firms, announcing that associate Harry Turnipseed has been made a partner at the firm. Rarely do I know of the associate, and sometimes I have a hard time placing the name of the firm. Such announcements go quickly into my circular file, a.k.a., the trash bin. I suspect that many other clients react the same way to these unsolicited mailings which clutter their in-boxes.

Why send these out to clients who have no knowledge of the newly-minted partner? Adjusting firms should draw some lessons from this, and avoid some of the follies of their lawyer counterparts.

Save time, postage and engraving costs in being selective in such announcements. Most adjusting company clients are awash in paper anyway, and this way you are simply adding to the clutter. If the announcement pertains to an adjuster with whom the client has worked, by all means send out an announcement. Otherwise, save the rainforest and spare a tree.

If you bring someone on staff who is seasoned, has some extra dimension in which clients would be interested, then by all means toot your (and their) horn. The appropriate forum for this should not be an engraved announcement, but rather something in your client newsletter (see section on newsletters). Or, draw up a brief letter to go out to your regular clients, touting the addition of someone new to your staff. You should also send the announcement to the appropriate periodicals.

If a trainee adjuster joins your staff, prepare an appropriate biography and profile that person in your client newsletter. As a matter of fact, it is a good idea to keep handy the biographies or c.v.'s of your professional claim staff. Consider putting them on a word processor or floppy disk, and updating regularly to stay current. This saves time in the long run and puts you at a competitive advantage. For insurance carriers, it can show and highlight the expertise of its claim staff vis a vis the competition. For independent adjusters, it can come in handy when bidding on a contract, or when the interested prospect says, "I'm intrigued, but would like to know more about your staff." Encourage your staff to update their company bios periodically — designations earned, courses taken, specialized training, articles written, speeches or presentations given, etc.

As you add to your staff and bring new people on board, give some thought as to the best way to notify clients. Tell them how this staffing addition or change enables you to serve them better. That is superior to sending out an engraved announcement.

Avoiding "Monday Madness"

Mondays are hell in claim departments, and they are often no exception for your client's office. For one thing, new loss reports are often streaming in from mishaps occurring over the weekend. Phones are jumping off the receivers from people who have waited all weekend for a check or payment, and are hopping mad when it did not arrive on Saturday! People call in sick with the flu, so you are short-handed. You start the week off, and feel behind the eight ball already. You wear a "I Hate Mondays" button, but it does no good. As Karen Carpenter sang, "Rainy days and Mondays always get you down."

> *Monday is a get-back-to work day. Most time management research has proven that Mondays are stress-filled and very busy. Consequently, you should avoid trying to put one more item on people's agendas. As a general rule, avoid Monday if you can.*
>
> —Paul Karasik "How to Make it Big In The Seminar Business," McGraw-Hill, 1992)

What is true for holding seminars on Monday also holds true for bugging clients. Mondays are hectic enough without you adding to the client's agenda. Then there's the mail. Monday mail is normally a two-day bulge consisting of Saturday and Monday mail. Hence, you get a double-dose of incoming letters, case assignments and demands to address. Mondays are rough and busy. If you think Mondays are tough for you, think of how they are for your client.

Therefore, avoid trying to schedule meetings with clients on Mondays. They will appreciate the thoughtfulness. In fact, it may be a good idea to avoid phoning the client on Mondays altogether, since they are liable to be preoccupied with the crisis of the moment. Other weekdays work best. On Tuesdays, the mail volume is lighter and people are settled into the week's work routine. On Fridays, people may be thinking more about the upcoming weekend or be more likely to take a vacation day. For "prime time" in contacting clients, the "interior" days of the week — Tuesday, Wednesday and Thursday — are better than Monday or Friday.

Unless the client specifically asks, avoid scheduling Monday visits, meetings, conferences or phone calls.

You've probably got extra work to do on Monday as well.

The Secrets to Keeping Clients

It is much harder to find new clients than to keep existing customers. Hence, time spent in taking the client's "satisfaction temperature" periodically is time well-spent, a worthy investment. Client relations are not static, but dynamic. They change — for better or for worse. They are not snapshots, but full-length feature films of undetermined length.

You must have the courage to put yourself on the line periodically and invite the client's candid, unvarnished feedback regarding the type of job you are doing for them. This goes beyond the merely superficial, "How are we doing?" or "Are you happy?" types of questions, though for openers those gambits are fine. Claim departments and service providers need to probe beyond the superficial, to see where they can make even the tiniest improvement in their claim service. Little by little, improve each day. To win, sometimes you do not have to hit home runs, only single after single. But you must always listen to your customers, even when they don't particularly want to talk.

In this section, you will learn some useful tips and tactics on how to draw them out, get them talking, and offer you opportunities to improve your service.

Survey Client Satisfaction: "Was It Good For You, Too?"

You may think you are doing a good job for your clients and that they are all happy. How do you really know, however? Do not give the time-worn answer, "Because we haven't had any/many complaints recently." Most disgruntled clients do not vocalize their discontent. They just quietly send their case assignments elsewhere.

Being a pizza lover, I order in delivery from Domino's, the "thirty-minute-or-else" people. For each pizza I order, Domino's sends me a detailed, two-page questionnaire, quizzing me on such matters as greasiness, amount of cheese, and whether there were too few or too many toppings. All of this for a $12 pizza. What does this have to do with claim service?

If Domino's is concerned about my purchase of a twelve-buck pizza, how much do I have to spend on a claim service before they ask me for feedback in a systematic way? This is a rhetorical question, but perhaps one which many clients are asking themselves.

When was the last time you surveyed your clients about how good a job you're doing for them?

Unfortunately, it is so easy to become immersed in the technicalities of case-handling that we forget to ask clients how we are doing. We assume that the absence of complaints is a sign that things are just fine. Maybe … but maybe not. In our zeal to tend to the "trees" of specific files, we must not lose sight of the "forest" of overall client satisfaction. One is a "micro" perspective and the other "macro."

In 1991, for instance, Crawford & Company began sending a service survey card on each and every claim file they handled for clients. It is printed on a self-addressed, postage-paid postcard for client convenience. This is a very positive step, but it is remarkable how few adjusting firms or claim services routinely survey their clients. Clients can be a gold-mine of suggestions which no in-house suggestion box would produce.

Send clients questionnaires when their cases have been closed. Client answers will provide valuable insights on how clients view your claims department or adjusting service. In addition to meeting with major clients at least annually, consider sending them a questionnaire as well. Meetings and questionnaires are also useful for getting referrals to potential clients. It amazes me still how little adjusting companies survey their clients for customer satisfaction, ideas or complaints.

My own company uses one large claims adjusting outfit across the nation for our product liability claims. Over the past three years, we have paid this firm over $2.2 million in outside claim adjusting fees. Not once have I ever received a customer satisfaction survey from this company. Due to conflict situations, occasionally we have to use this company's chief competitor, headquartered in the South.

Recently, we paid a $500 service bill to the second company and received a postage-paid customer satisfaction survey. The adjusting service to whom I was paying close to a million dollars a year did not seem interested in surveying me, yet the other company was interested in how I felt about a $500 service invoice. Now, don't misunderstand, the adjusting company I currently use doesn't need to mail me a questionnaire in order to know how I feel about their service. We hold regular account review meetings, have an electronic mail (E-mail) hookup and are quite vocal. Still, I felt somewhat taken for granted and was struck by the disparity of treatment. Perhaps if more adjusting companies surveyed their clients, they would improve trust, improve their relationships, and learn ways to improve their businesses.

1. **Take your clients' temperatures periodically.** Regularly ask clients how well you are doing and in what other ways you can help them. Ask them during cases, when they are over, or at billing time. This shows you really care about whether they are satisfied. How will you ever know if your clients are satisfied unless you ask them? There is no improvement without feedback. Do NOT assume that no news is good news. Do not think that an absence of complaints means everything is OK.

2. **Provide the option of anonymity.** You are much more likely to obtain candid responses if you allow clients the option to remain anonymous. Some may be reluctant to tell you of their displeasure, but will offer their unvarnished opinions if the survey does allow them to omit their names.

3. **Consider developing the questionnaire form in-house.** Law firms can spend thousands of dollars paying consultants to develop surveys. In my view, however, most law firms can put together an effective survey tapping their own talent. It is far from being the model of perfection, but my own company developed the survey on the following page, which can be adapted to the needs of many organizations.

4. **Make sure your medium doesn't undercut your message.** The mere act of conducting a survey telegraphs a message to your clients: that you care about them and their opinions of your work. This is not to say that the survey should be window dressing. Our company recently received a client satisfaction survey from a Kansas law firm we use for product liability defense work. The cover letter was addressed to our claims manager, but misspelled that person's name. While we were happy to receive a client survey form, misspelling the client's name sends a mixed

CLAIM SERVICE SURVEY

Claim: _____ **vs.** _____

Recently, the above claim was closed. By way of follow-up, we would like to assess your impressions of the quality of our claim service. The quality of claim service that you receive from XYZ Corporation, our adjusting firm and selected defense lawyers is of the utmost importance to us. We aim to provide the best possible claim service, but we look to you, our members, for an evaluation of that service.

Please take a few minutes to complete this form and return it to us in the self-addressed, stamped envelope. We appreciate your feedback, including any concerns or suggestions.

1. How would you rate the claim service you received from XYZ Corporation?
   ☐ Very Good ☐ Good ☐ Adequate ☐ Poor
   If you replied "Poor" please explain. _____

2. How would you rate our claim service compared to other claim services?
   ☐ Much better ☐ Better ☐ As good ☐ Not as good

3. With 1 being the lowest and 5 being the highest how would you rate our adjuster in these areas?

Knowledgeable	1	2	3	4	5
Cooperative	1	2	3	4	5
Accessible	1	2	3	4	5
Attentive to your needs	1	2	3	4	5

4. On this particular claim, how would you rate the service you received from XYZ?
   ☐ Very Good ☐ Good ☐ Adequate ☐ Poor
   If you replied "Poor" please explain. _____

5. How would you rate the overall service you received from your defense attorney?
   ☐ Very Good ☐ Good ☐ Adequate ☐ Poor
   If you replied "Poor" please explain. _____

6. With 1 being the lowest and 5 being the highest how would you rate counsel selected by XYZ?

Expertise	1	2	3	4	5
Cooperation	1	2	3	4	5
Accessibility	1	2	3	4	5
Attention to your needs	1	2	3	4	5

7. Rate your interest level in participating or attending the following:
   Defense/Claim Seminars
   ☐ Very Interested ☐ Interested ☐ Not Interested
   Risk Management Seminars
   ☐ Very Interested ☐ Interested ☐ Not Interested

8. What could we do to improve our Claim Service? _____
   _____

Thank you for taking the time to complete this form. Your response will enable us to continue to grow and improve the quality of service we provide.

message: "We care enough to survey your views, but we don't care enough to make sure we spell your name right." Make sure that your medium does not undercut your message.

Our office received a service survey from a Midwestern law firm. The envelope to our national claims coordinator misspelled her name in a hideous fashion. She laughed about it, but was tempted to tell the firm that they'd be much better off just getting her name right than in paying thousands of dollars to an outside consultant and pollster. Though her attitude was jocular, deep down she was irked by the inattention. It was like getting a Christmas card saying, "Dear Occupant, We very much appreciate your business …" A quibbling point? Perhaps. However your hours and thousands of dollars can go down the drain with a simple "minor" mistake such as this.

> *Quinley's Client Relations Rule Number 76: Get the client's name right, at least.*

5. **Acknowledge responses and thank identified recipients.** Unless you acknowledge client responses promptly, they may infer that your survey was all show and no substance. In advance of addressing any criticism, thank your clients for completing the survey. This is basic courtesy. Your clients are busy too and carved time out of their schedules to complete the questionnaire.

6. **Follow up on complaints quickly and close the loop.** Strive to acknowledge the complaint, or anything bordering on a complaint, within 24 hours. Set a time limit for acknowledging the complaint, and another for responding to it. Act quickly. Try to provide a response in, say, seven calendar days. When the trail gets cold, the client gets the stronger impression that you don't care.

7. **Scan the totality of responses for general trends.** Some business consultants say that you should love complaints, because they give you an opportunity to improve. Few business people — claim professionals included — love complaints. Yet there is some truth to this notion. What is it about your claim service

that bugs clients? Late reports? Failure to follow directions? Lack of technical expertise? Adjuster turnover? Billing errors? Runaway expenses? Failure to communicate? Identify the service sore points which surveys reveal, and you will have a weather vane, pointing you in the direction where your corrective focus should lie.

8. **Take corrective action.** You've acknowledged the client's concern. You've addressed it with the client. Now is the time to address it within your organization. Follow up and take corrective action. Establish reporting guidelines and track staff progress. Redouble efforts at staff training to enhance expertise of the claim staff. Re-examine your billing practices and format if those are sore points. Beware of shrugging off client complaints with the attitude, "That client is an idiot." If clients think you have a problem, then whether you agree or not, you have a problem. In service areas, such as claims adjusting and servicing, perception quickly becomes reality.

9. **Tabulate results, re-survey and track findings and progress from year to year.**

10. **Don't just ask clients, "Are you satisfied?"** Go one step further and ask, "How can we serve you better?"

Surveys do not have to be in a written form in order to be effective. At Caronia Corporation, a specialty claims outfit headquartered on Long Island, New York, all clients are placed on a 30-day phone diary. Someone from the company calls the client once a month to ask, "What could we do to improve our service?" The persons making these calls are different from the people handling the files. These "temperature-taking" calls are not claim file-specific. It is also made clear to the clients that the callers are not "checking up on the adjusters" in Big Brother fashion, and that no one will get reprimanded. It is simply a way to determine what is on the minds of the clients.

Charles Caronia, CEO of Caronia Corporation, states that clients might take this opportunity to suggest a different invoicing schedule or format, complain that adjusters arrive unannounced, or to suggest that everything is just all right. Caronia uses this systematic telephone outreach to dispel the impression that once a client is signed on, the marketing people simply move on to new prospects.

Hold an Annual
Client Service Retreat

Plan a Client Service Retreat once a year and have present all the people who have daily contact with clients. Some suggestions for a well-run client service retreat:

1. **Plan ahead.** The more planning you do, the better investment of time you will have. A successful retreat is not a vacation junket, but requires considerable advance work.

2. **Go off-site.** Holding such a meeting in your office violates the concept of what a retreat is all about and misses the point. If you try to do this in your office, or in a conference room, there will be too many distractions: telephones, drop-in visitors, the emergency du jour. Part of the idea of a retreat is to, well, *retreat.* That is, get off site. Rent a cabin, a hotel meeting room, or ask your travel agent to book you in a nearby conference center. The idea is for people to get away from the trees for a day or two so that they can see the forest.

3. **Give some thought to attendance.** All people who service clients should be invited. You may have to close down the office for one day. If you explain to customers in advance the reason for this, i.e. exploring was you can serve them better, they may understand and fully support the idea.

Another radical idea: Give some thought to inviting a client along to the retreat. Offer to pick up their expenses. Ask them to share ideas that they may have on how to improve claim service. Give the customer a voice at the retreat. Some ideas which sound great around a conference table may have no added value to a client. On the other hand, a client may be able to isolate an area of needed service improvement which the claim staff could overlook.

4. **Have a detailed agenda planned and circulate it in advance.** This means at least two weeks prior to the event. The more lead time you allow for preparation, the more "return" you will get from the effort.

5. **Ask each person, in advance, to prepare some remarks on (a) new ways to improve client service and (b) resources — capital, financial, personnel — needed to attain those objectives.** Obviously, all services have costs, but now is not the time to kill ideas in their infancy.

6. **Remember, it's a retreat.** Attendees should feel free to bring their swim suit or tennis racquets, as long as they know this will be a *working* retreat, with some unstructured time for R&R. Build some time into the schedule for rest and recreation. Do not jam-pack the schedule so tightly that people have no "down time." This is a key part of a retreat: unstructured time during which people can relax, reflect and think. Isn't that what you want them to do? Schedule some social activities into the agenda.

7. **Brainstorm for ideas.** Do not judge or shoot any down. The time for final evaluation of ideas can come later, after the retreat. This is not the time to greet new ideas with that innovation-killing mantra, "It's not in the budget."

8. **Before the retreat is over, prior to adjournment, compile a list of "action points" for follow up.** One problem of retreats is that people get inspired during the brief time they are on one, but the initiatives started later get lost in the crush of day to day work flow. Before you leave the meeting room or conference facility, have an assignment of follow-up items, who will do what,

and some target date for completion or follow up.

9. **Follow up.** Capitalize on the momentum and inspiration generated by the retreat. A common problem is that, during retreats, people think of wonderful ideas, then the meeting adjourns and everyone goes back to business as usual. This renders the retreat a waste of time. There must be concrete follow-up from a customer service retreat in order to implement strategies to deliver real value to adjusting company clients. Schedule a follow-up meeting within 30 days, in your office, to gauge progress in implementing customer service improvements.

The annual retreat can be an effective tool toward "keeping the pot stirred," inspiring your claim staff to generate ideas on how to improve claim service and keep every client happy.

Do Your Homework
on the Client

You will flunk if you don't do your homework. What is true in school is true in Claim Service Real World 101 as well. Before meeting with or "pitching" your business or services to a client, learn all you can about the prospect. This is fundamental in doing your homework. According to sales consultant Jonathan Whitcup of Consultative Resources Corp. of Darien, Connecticut, one way to sabotage a client call is to not worry about preparation. He calls this "elevator planning," when the caller starts thinking about what he's going to say as he steps into the elevator (*Success*, May 1992, "Five Ways to Sabotage Your Sales," p. 20). Do not succumb to "elevator preparation." It only goes one way — down, not up.

There is certain required reading which enters into getting and keeping any client. Here are the recommended "homework" texts:

1. **The Annual Report.** Request a copy. Read it in advance of your visit to or meeting with the client. Prepare a few questions from the annual report to demonstrate to the client that you have actually read the annual report with some thought and care. If the prospect is a privately-held company, such information may not be available. Still, probe to see if there is any ad-

vance information you can obtain from the company. Just by asking shows that you have given the company some thought and is likely to impress the prospect.

2. **Guidelines for outside adjusting services.** Whatever these are called, more and more clients are developing such guidelines. They may be bound in a three-ring binder or be more informal. Ask the client or prospective client if they have any written guidelines for outside adjusters. If so, request a copy and read these closely. Again, prepare some questions.

More and more clients are developing their own written case-handling guidelines for outside adjusters and third-party administrators. Get used to it. Whether claim professionals like this or not, the trend is likely to continue.

3. **Client newsletter.** See if the client has a newsletter, even if it's one they circulate primarily internally. The client's newsletter may give some insight into their "corporate culture" and what they are all about as a company. Ask if you can be added to the mailing list.

4. **Read/review open claims.** Before visiting an existing client, it should go without saying that you should read and review the open cases that your firm currently has with that client. Time allowing, it might also be a good idea to review some recently-closed cases. Make sure you are conversant with these cases. If the claims are too voluminous to do this, consider preparing a case-by-case summary or digest for your ready reference. This digest should include: the claimant's name, brief description of loss, reserves and payments to date, current status.

My company had a memorable encounter with one large well-known New Orleans defense law firm. We were experiencing some service problems: late reports, unreturned phone calls, billing snags, etc. Our national claims coordinator visited the firm's partner who had been "handling" these cases. We were astonished to learn that:

- The attorney had not bothered to pull any of the open cases that we had currently pending with that firm.

- The attorney had not read these files in preparation or anticipation of our visit.
- The attorney professed not to know that we had written litigation guidelines for outside counsel, even though these accompany the assignment with each new case.

To worsen matters, this same firm later sent another, more senior partner to our office, presumably to "patch things up."

Wrong!

The senior partner was unprepared to discuss specific cases, specific case-handling and servicing problems and was unaware of our prior complaints. It was clear that his visit to our office was intended — in his mind — to be an atmospheric social call. The firm still enjoys an impressive reputation, notwithstanding our hideous experience from their service.

Our account and business could have been salvaged by this firm, had they simply done their homework.

That law firm is now on our company's list of *previously* approved counsel. There is a lesson here for all service providers, particularly those in the claim adjusting field. While this anecdote deals with a law firm, the lesson should not be lost on claim service providers. The Boy Scout motto of "Be Prepared" works well here. Just by doing your homework and preparing, you will set yourself apart from 90 percent of your competitors.

Find out not only about the company, but also about the person you will be meeting or dealing with. Find out who the real decision-makers are. Be discreet in your inquiries. Ask your counterparts at other companies, or mutual acquaintances who know the person that will be your contact. Try to develop a profile of the person, particularly if you have not met him or her before. Whether you are preparing to meet a prospect for the first time, or are meeting a new client, try to learn as much about them as you can in advance. Some things to learn:

- Experience in the job. Are they newly-promoted, or have they been with the same company for many years? Are they new to the company?

- Vocational background. Is the client a finance-numbers type, or is their background from the insurance or claims area?
- Educational background. Is the client an MBA, lawyer, college grad? Where did they attend school? Maybe you can find some affinity and common ground here.
- Negotiating style. Hard-nosed or laid-back?
- Personality. Low key or type triple-A? Abrasive or charming?
- Pet peeves. Everybody has likes and dislikes. Try to learn the client's (or prospective client's) "hot buttons" so the two of you will be in synch.

In claims adjusting, success goes to those who are prepared. Quizzes are not given for this kind of homework. In lieu of straight A's, adjusting services get their gilded report card in the form of new business, repeat assignments and satisfied customers.

16 Questions That Show a Client You Care

Claims professionals like to talk, and are usually pretty skilled at it. It's tougher to sit still and listen, though. You can astonish the client — in a pleasant way — by asking open-ended questions and listening to the answers. Capitalize on the fact that the client enjoys telling you about his or her organization. Here are the questions clients love to hear from outside adjusting services, particularly those who are seeking new business:

1. **"Tell me about your company."** How can adjusters presume to know how to service a client's business unless they understand the client's business? And how can they understand the client's business unless they ask the client to educate them a little bit? Moral: Ask!

2. **"What differentiates you from other companies in your market?** Do not assume that all companies, or clients, are alike. This is no more valid than assuming that all adjusting companies are the same. Each company — in any field — has something which they feel sets them apart from their competition. Some companies specialize by line of coverage, others by commercial versus personal lines, other by geographic area, some by insuring a particular industry. It's always interesting to hear a company explain exactly how it differentiates itself from its com-

petition. Incidentally, it's an interesting question to put to adjusting firms as well, but we will return to this issue later.

3. **"What do you look for in outside adjusters?"** Never assume that all client needs are the same. You cannot keep clients happy unless you ask them what they want. Ask the client what they want. And then give it to them, just the way they want it.

4. **"What drives you crazy about outside adjusters and adjusting services?"** The answer to this will help you avoid stepping on land-mines. Get to know their pet peeves and "hot buttons" ahead of time. For example, some clients want loads of paper, some want reports only when there is something new to say. Some favor a team of adjusters working on a case. Others want strong accountability with one person handling all aspects of the claim. Best to find this out early on.

5. **"Exactly who within your office has the authority to select outside adjusters?"** Make sure you are talking to the decision-maker. Nothing is more deflating than delivering your best pitch, only to find out that the wrong person is in the batter's box! Make sure the person you talk with has authority to assign cases or to add new entries to their approved list of adjusters!

6. **"On what basis or criteria are outside adjusters selected?"** Listen closely. How heavily do "connections" enter in? For example, is there subtle or not-so-subtle pressure to use a company because a claims manager is a golfing buddy with some VIP? Does the client pick the cheapest service provider, or the one with the lowest hourly rate?

7. **"What problems have you had with outside adjusting services in the past?"** Without naming names. This is another way to avoid trouble. In my experience, very few adjusting services ask this question.

8. **"What claims volume do you have, overall and in my geographic area?"** This gives you some idea as to the size of the pie in your area. How hard do you want to market if the total volume of assignments averages two per year? Is that the best investment of your company's time?

9. **"What do we have to do to get case assignments from you?"** A time-honored sales technique: Ask for the order! Even very few marketing types ask this question. You would be surprised how often the direct and forthright approach succeeds. This does not mean being high-pressure, though.

10. **"How would you describe your company's claim philosophy?"** Is each case a diamond in the rough, or is the prospect mainly interested in getting cases closed and behind them? How heavily does the precedent factor of settlements weigh in their decisions? How closely do they want to be involved in the claims process? Are they very risk-averse, or are they willing to roll the dice on defending large exposure cases?

11. **"How do you feel about 'nuisance' settlements?"** Some organizations love them, some tolerate them and some loathe them. Best to know this before recommending, "Your insured has zero liability, but to curb defense costs we suggest considering a $5,000 nuisance-value settlement."

12. **"How do you feel about a 'team approach' to defending cases?"** Better know this before you start staffing a file with one general adjuster, two inside adjusters, and a claim support assistant. Some clients are skeptical toward the team approach, believing that it is a prescription for duplication, multiple billing, redundant billing, inefficiency and lack of accountability.

13. **"How is your business doing these days?"** This also gives you some idea about prospective claim volume. If business is down, the law of averages would imply that potential claim assignments will also be low. A healthy growth rate implies the potential for additional adjusting needs.

14. **"With what other companies would you compare yourself?"** Seek a frame of reference. While each company prides itself on being unique, who would they most closely resemble?

15. **"Do you see any changes in using outside adjusters?"** More and more companies are experimenting with bringing the adjusting function in-house, to save money. Insurers and self-insureds feel tremendous pressure to find ways to trim costs, and

have to fight the financial types who see this strictly as a dollars and cents issue. A few clients have established "captive" adjusting firms which function similar to a regular outfit but handle only those cases generated by its own operations. The answer to this question can give you some insight as to whether the insurer is going to bring cases in-house, which obviously could impact the odds of you getting any assignments.

16. **"What other risk management needs does your company have, outside of claim investigation?"** Do not overlook other markets for your services or pass up business opportunities. If the client is not interested in you adjusting claims, how about handling their damage appraisals, litigation management, pre-loss inspection reports, etc. If you are interested in becoming a full service firm, perhaps you can get your foot in the door in some other fashion. Lay the groundwork for a broader business relationship. If you define your business scope in too narrow terms, you may forego other lucrative opportunities.

Show a broad business interest beyond the narrow confines of the insurance, claims and adjusting world. This by itself will help elevate you from your competition, in the eyes of prospects and clients.

Client Remembrances: "We'll Always Have Paris"

Find out the client's secretary's birthday and send a birthday card or remembrance of some kind. Make friends within all client levels — up and down the corporate pecking order. Another tip: don't forget the client's birthday. Some service firms keep a stock of cards on hand ready to go out at a moment's notice.

In addition, send out short notes of congratulations to business people you know who have been promoted or who have joined another company. If you find out they won a trial or a big account, drop them a congratulatory note. If they have been named in the trade press in a favorable light, take time to mention this praiseworthy event. This is a little extra which tells the clients you are thinking of them and are proud to have them as a client.

You never know when one of these people will be in a position to hire you or your adjusting firm, or at least recommend you to someone who is looking to move their business elsewhere. You never know where people will pop up. Do not burn any bridges if you can help it.

Try to remember names of family members, special interests or hobbies, and other personal information about clients. Whenever possible, send congratulatory cards and letters on special occasions. For example, I regularly scan the *Wall Street Journal, Business Week* and *Fortune* magazine for mention of one of my company's clients. Since we provide liability insurance coverage to medical device companies, much of the news about our clients is poor — FDA seizures, recalls, lawsuits, medical safety concerns, etc.

On the other hand, biotechnology is a "hot" field, and many times there are favorable articles on a device company's management, FDA clearance, innovative products, initial public offering, stock and financial performance, etc. I never fail to clip one of these positive articles and send it to the client with a brief congratulatory cover note. The note always concludes by stating how proud we are to have them as a client in our MEDMARC program. A little touch like this, by itself, will likely not cement an account relationship. However, the next time one of our competitors is making a sales pitch to that company, I'm hoping and betting they will remember that gesture and not be lured away by a cheaper premium. It is one little factor, an intangible admittedly, which I feel will work in our company's favor and make us stand out from the competition.

> *Quinley's Corollary #82 of Client Service: Yesterday's mail clerk can become tomorrow's CEO. Big trees grow from little nuts.*

Client Quirks

Learn your clients' quirks and idiosyncrasies. Be a student of their likes and dislikes. Study clients the way an ornithologist would study a rare bird. Some companies will get upset when you charge them one-tenth of an hour's work or for photocopying one or two pages. Some may feel insulted if your receptionist does not instantly recognize their voice. Others go ballistic if their phone calls are screened. Some view their claims as befitting the treatment of rare antiques. Other clients view claims like crates on a loading dock, "Let's get these mothers moving and outta' here!"

John Nelson, an executive with Countrywide Services in St. Louis, believes that many clients have "hot buttons," which set them off. He believes adjusting firms should never press any of the following "hot buttons":
- Lack of confidentiality.
- Late reporting.
- Failure to follow up.
- Costs inconsistent with results.
- No recommendations offered.
- Inadequate or incorrect reserving.
The latter is particularly important for self-insured contract

accounts, where the claim service functions de facto as the client's claim department. GIGO — Garbage In, Garbage Out — applies here. A mis-stated reserve or a loss allocated to the wrong division can skew financial statements or knock a plant manager out of a bonus. Think how THAT will make the client feel!

You may think you know enough about your clients. Chances are, you should think again. Take a look at Harvey Mackay's 66-question client checklist in his book, "Swim With the Sharks Without Being Eaten Alive," (pages 28-34). The level of detail that Mackay's company seeks in profiling clients is astounding — everything from their college affiliation to the names of their spouses. All this for an envelope company! If an envelope company feels this is important, how much more client-centered should be those service organizations who handle something as sensitive as claims?

Consider using or adapting Mackay's checklist to your adjusting clients. Learn your client's quirks and tiptoe around them. The better you know your clients, the better chance you have to hold on to them. Make it your business.

Ask Why You're
Not Getting Cases

If you're an independent adjusting firm or claims management outfit, and you are not getting assignments from clients who used to send you cases, or if you know those cases are going to other firms, ask the client about it. Be diplomatic, but ask clients,

"Why haven't I received an assignment from you recently?"

"Is everything OK between us?"

"Are you satisfied with our service?"

Be willing to put yourself on the line. John Nelson, Countrywide Services, St. Louis, Missouri, comments, "We know not all clients will be happy and satisfied at all times. They key is knowing when there is dissatisfaction and how quickly we react."

Most customers receiving poor service do not complain. For every overt complaint, you can be sure there are more disgruntled customers with negative feelings they have not voiced. Many people with gripes do not complain because it is inconvenient, takes too much time, or they don't think it will do any good. For whatever reason many clients do not complain, even when they are less than totally satisfied. Do not infer that everything is great simply because your clients voice no complaints. Some will discretely take their business elsewhere. Moral: Make it easy for client to give you constructive criticism. Open the client's suggestion box, and use them as a partner for improving your service.

Maybe "complain" is a bad word. It certainly has negative connotations. See these remarks not as complaints but more as "opportunities for service improvements." Turn a negative into a positive. It seems like very few adjusting firms are doing this. Be prepared for some bracing replies, though. In some cases, a client may take this opportunity to vent years of displeasure. Why hasn't the client voiced this before? Perhaps you didn't ask! (See the section on client satisfaction surveys.)

Maybe the client will let you know that there have been no recent claims in your area. In this situation, there may be little alternative than to relocate to Los Angeles, Cook or Dade counties!

In other situations, you may find that you are no longer talking to the client's decision-maker. Perhaps there has been some change or turnover among the risk management staff, or the person who used to assign you cases has moved on to another company. In this case, you can refine your avenue for pursuing business.

In still other cases, you may learn that another adjusting firm has undercut your rates. You may decide that you do not want to compete on price, but at least you will have an opportunity to make this decision yourself. The point is that if you want to know why you are not getting new business, you may have to ask. Clients are unlikely to announce to you the reasons, unless they are extremely discontent. Even then, customer surveys have shown that only a small percentage of disgruntled customers complain. Most just quietly take their business elsewhere.

In sales training, students are told to "close" by coming right out and asking for the order. Adjusters may shrink from this, because of the notion that in their profession they need not stoop to salesmanship.

Forget about it. The direct approach can pay dividends. Sometimes you have to ask for the business. Do not go so overboard that you become a pest. Keep track of the assignments you are getting from major clients. Tabulate these on a month-to-month or quarter-to-quarter basis. If you see a significant dip, then follow up. There's not much you can do to increase claims, though independent adjusters in some regions have been known to pray for hurricanes, floods and other natural disasters. You never want the client to get the impression that you wish they had more claims. While more files might be your livelihood, they are the client's anathema. If the client says he's not getting claims because he's having fewer accidents, take the opportunity to compliment his company's loss prevention services. To the extent loss prevention succeeds, there may be fewer claims.

If you find a client who is very happy with your service but does not have any assignments to give, see if you can get permission to use that client as a reference for other prospects. The client might even be willing to give a testimonial which you can use in some of your promotional literature.

Cost Effectiveness

C lients are increasingly strapped to meet or reduce their budgets. This can constrain the amount of money and discre-
tion they have to refer cases to outside adjusters and adjusting
services. All the more reason why we as adjusting firms must give
them outstanding reasons to use us. The reality is, however, that
Cadillac service may not be appealing if it is not cost effective.
Quality includes cost-effectiveness.

   As a point of discussion, here are some creative ways you can
serve as partners with your clients in the battle against rising
costs. Finding ways to SAVE your client's money becomes an
extra dimension of value-added service which keeps clients coming back to you time and time again.

19 Ways to Avoid Billing Blues

In these cost-sensitive times, clients are scrutinizing billings more closely than ever. The potential for billing problems to spoil relations between the claim service provider and the client looms large. All is not lost, though. Here are nineteen suggestions on how to avoid billing problems:

1. **Do not overlook the obvious.** Do good work cheap. Well, at least do good work at reasonable cost. This is really what all clients want.

2. **Do not be misled by hourly rates.** Realize that hourly rates are a deceptive index of cost or efficiency. Cost equals hourly rate times number of hours worked. "Cheaper" adjusters with lower hourly rates are no bargain if they take twice as long to complete certain tasks. It does little good to lure a client with low hourly rates, only to have bills get padded through inefficiency. Make sure that adjusters are not compensating for the low hourly rate by adding their own "loading" factors when they charge.

3. **Do not dismiss hourly rates, either.** Having said that, hourly rates are not irrelevant, though. They are one index of cost. The other index is the amount of time charged per task. An experienced adjuster, billing $75 per hour, may be able to finish an

investigation in half the time it takes an adjuster with a $45 dollar an hour rate. In this case, it pays for the client to look beyond the hourly rate, to the efficiency of adjusters. The problem is that years of experience may not necessarily correlate to greater efficiency. One would like to think so, but it is not always the case. A ten-year adjuster may simply be a one-year adjuster ten times over. The client sees the hourly rate up front. The client sees the amount charged per task only at the end, after the fact, by which time it is a fait accompli. By the time the client sees how much was charged per task, it may be too late. For this reason alone, clients tend to focus, somewhat myopically at times, on hourly rate.

4. **Prepare budgets.** On serious claims, prepare a claim plan and budget within 90 days of assignment, even if the client does not request or require it. (See the next chapter for a sample claim investigative plan and budget.) This will accomplish a number of objectives. It will impress the client and send a message that you too are concerned about costs. Further, you have just made it easier for the client to set a reserve on the case. Third, you have just helped the client make the defend-or-settle decision so key to case management.

Case investigation and defense is dynamic, and situations change rapidly. That is why updating the claim plan and budget is key, because their shelf-life is so brief.

Merely preparing an investigative plan and budget, unbidden by the client, will set you apart from 99 percent of the other adjusting firms. It is also a good discipline to impose on yourself.

5. **Keep your budget and plan current.** Update the investigative plan and budget regularly thereafter — at least every six months and preferably every quarter. Because exigencies change during the life of the claim, budgets must be recalibrated periodically. What started out looking like a minor claim may blossom into an extensive claim or assignment. What appeared at first to be a serious claim may turn out to be not so severe or taxing.

6. **Explain budget variances.** Explain in advance any deviations in the budget. Keep an eye on the meter. Budgets are not contracts and they are not written in stone. They should not be flypaper, either. If your work has significantly exceeded the budget, you ought to preempt criticism by bringing the client's attention to it or explaining the unavoidable reasons why you are running over budget. Moreover, take that opportunity to provide the client with an updated/revised budget, and try to stick to it.

7. **Practice preventive measures.** Review bills before they go out to the client. It is surprising the number of legal bills, audited on a random basis, which contain gross or obvious errors indicating zero bill review. These include but are not limited to: arithmetic errors (never, it seems, in the client's interest), stray charges from unrelated files, etc.

8. **Watch your charges.** Do NOT charge the client for this bill review. Straightening out bills or explaining them is a cost of doing business. No client expects to be charged for this, as if getting a billing problem resolved is some type of "frill." Incredibly, I have seen adjusting companies charge for this, which only incenses clients further. In addition, there should be no charges for routine bill review which, presumably, claim supervisors ought to be doing anyway.

9. **Publicize voluntary bill reductions.** If you reduce a bill voluntarily, on a preemptive basis, let the client know. You might be able to preempt a bill complaint if you demonstrate your concern for costs. If, in response to a bill complaint, you begin itemizing work for which you did not charge, the gesture will seem somewhat suspect and self-serving. Briefly detailing the work that was not billed sends a comforting message to the client: that you are keeping an eye on the meter.

10. **Demonstrate your cost-sensitivity.** If you or your office performed work for which you did not charge the client, let the client know. This claim will have more credibility now than it would in response to a bill complaint.

11. **Be open-minded.** Be open to discussion and reason on fee questions. Do not get defensive if clients question your bills. This comes with the territory. Few service firms can afford not to be open to discussing fees. Granted, there are those few and far between clients who habitually challenge every bill. If this is the case, ask yourself whether you really want to do business with a company like this. Such is the exception, though. A poorly-handled response to a bill inquiry can turn a merely peeved client into a *former* client.

12. **Do not charge for time spent untangling billing snafus.** Do NOT charge the client for straightening out billing problems. Incredibly, I have received bills from local branch adjusting offices for engaging in back-and-forth with their home office regarding some billing snafu. I have never paid such a charge, nor should any client. If a merchant made an error in your bill, would they think of charging you for the "privilege" of straightening it out?

13. **Watch the details.** Read the client's billing guidelines. Adhere to them. If the client has gone to the trouble of developing some written guidelines, make sure you read and adhere to them. More and more clients have their own guidelines. Get used to it.

14. **Promote pro-rating.** Make sure work and billings are pro-rated among clients. If your adjusters work on more than one case — as they should — per trip, make sure that such time is pro-rated among all the clients. This way, the savings is passed on to the client and the adjuster makes one trip accomplish a number of objectives — a true win-win outcome.

15. **When in doubt, get client approval for big ticket expenses.** Get client pre-approval for significant expenditures. Before undertaking an IME with a specialist, engaging an accident reconstruction expert or paying hundreds of dollars for a professional photographer, get the client's approval. This avoids leaving you holding the bag, or the client disavowing such charges, claiming that you exceeded the bounds of your authority.

16. **Make bills easy on the eye.** Provide the client with bills which are user-friendly. Avoid "paragraph" or cluster billing, which lists a cluster of tasks and then, out to the side, reads, "For services rendered." Bills should be itemized, preferably in tenth-of-an-hour increments. The bills should be concise, understandable and easy to read.

17. **"Profit" is not a four-letter word.** You deserve a reasonable profit. You may have to "fire" an occasional client. I knew of one New Orleans claim office which had to part company with a major Northeast insurance carrier after that insurer refused to pay the firm more than $45 per hour. The firm had decided it simply could no longer make a profit at $45 an hour and requested a fee increase. When the carrier turned the firm down, the adjusters made a conscious economic decision to part company with that client. Each adjusting firm must decide on its own if the terms imposed or offered by an insurance carrier are realistic or penurious.

18. **Do not bill for overhead items.** Do not charge the client for items which are properly office overhead. Word processing fees, secretarial overtime, etc. — these are overhead expenses which should be built into your hourly cost structure, not unbundled and billed to the client. Increasingly, clients who purchase outside legal services are balking at paying for items they perceive as being overhead. Expect them to react the same way to adjusting bills including comparable items.

19. **Feel the need for speed!** Quicker resolution of cases = more assignments in the long run. It is an adage in claims adjusting that claims, unlike fine wine, do not improve with age. In general, if you can resolve cases faster, you will save the client adjusting fees and other related costs. This will garner you more assignments in the long run.

Be Price- and Cost-Sensitive

This is the era of the frugal client. Expenses for outside adjusting services add up fast. You will win clients over and keep them loyal if you adhere to the following habits:

1. **Make bills clear.** All time-and-expense bills should be itemized and legible, showing the client:

- The work that was done: This can be descriptive, such as "Insured statement" or keyed to some type of code.
- Who did it: Which adjuster, preferably by name, or at least the initials. Or, the adjusting company may have an employee code. The client should have some type of key or legend which tells them the names of everyone who has billed on a file.
- How long it took: self-explanatory.
- Hourly rate of the person doing the work: In some adjusting companies, hourly rate varies by experience level. More seasoned adjusters may command higher hourly rates, but they may be more efficient. Neophyte adjusters may bill at a lower rate, but are slower and less efficient by virtue of their inexperience.

Itemized bills should be clear and legible. Nowadays there is little excuse for adjusting firms being unable to generate computerized T&E bills. The client should not have to slog through ten pages of a hand-written bill itemization sheet. The bill should be reasonably user friendly. Look at attorney bills. You may blanch at the amounts on them, but they are normally readable. Adjusting firms who provide hand-written bills might as well take statements with quill and inkwell and ride to appointments on horseback.

2. **Avoid games in charging.** Bill for actual time, not in "unit costs." Most clients are comfortable with billing for actual time spent, unless gross inefficiencies are present. Clients often balk at paying hidden unit costs, such as each page of a signed statement being billed at .5 hours, even when it takes few adjusters thirty minutes to take one page of statement.

3. **Slice the time thinly.** Bill in tenth-of-an-hour increments. Most clients are used to this from law firms. There may be a few adjusting (as well as law) firms which bill in fifteen-minute increments. Beware: if you cannot find a way to change your billing system into six minute slices, the client may find a way to change service providers.

4. **Go easy on the billing pencil.** Don't overwork files. Sharpen your pencil. A common billing complaint among clients is that adjusters go crazy in laying charges to the file, spin wheels and generally run up the tab. Every T&E service bill should be reviewed by a supervisor, if not a manager, before leaving the office or claim department. Such time in reviewing bills should NOT be charged back to the client.

5. **Review staffing decisions.** Be sure that case staffing makes economic sense. High-exposure cases should not go to trainee adjusters. First-party losses with low damages should not be assigned to experienced field adjusters. If you are going to send a trainee out to travel with a field adjuster to "learn the ropes," be careful about billing that. Clients may balk at paying for anyone's on the job training. If you are going to break a file up among two or more adjusters, parcelling out investigative or work assignments, then give some thought to whether that

makes economic sense for the client.

6. **Provide itemizations** of expenses with receipts. Not only should time be itemized, preferably in tenths-of-an-hour increments, but expenses should also be itemized. Backup documentation in the form of receipts should be submitted to the client.

7. **Set the ground rules on billing frequency.** Clarify billing intervals up front. If you bill open files monthly, quarterly or semi-annually, let the client know up front. Further, some adjusting companies raise their hourly fees from one billing period to another, without notifying clients. This is unwise. Whenever effecting a billing change, let the client know ahead of time. If all T&E files, for example, are to be billed at the same time — regardless of the age of the file — this may be useful for the client for budgeting purposes. Moral: tell the client the frequency with which you interim bill.

8. **Pay close attention to client bill procedures.** Read client billing guidelines carefully, and abide by them. If a client takes the time to write some guidelines, you ought to invest some time in reading — and heeding — them.

9. **Watch the meter on outside service providers you pick on the client's behalf.** Select outside service providers — contractors, counsel, copying services, rental car firms, etc. — for cost effectiveness.

10. **Provide context for your bills.** Let the client know:
- if you performed work for which you did not bill.
- if you preemptively reduced the bill.
- if there are any other special considerations that they should know about the bill.

11. **Ease off on "read and review" charges.** Just because some clients will pay for lawyers to do this does not mean that they will pay for an adjuster to do it. This may not be fair, but it is reality.

12. **Don't bill for untangling billing problems!** Clients do not want to be invoiced for the time you may spend reviewing bills or straightening out billing snafus. Put yourself in the client's shoes. If, for instance you took your TV in to an appliance shop

for repairs and they screwed up the bill, would you be willing to pay for the "service" of getting the mistake straightened out? Customers and clients expect a modicum of quality control and bill checking as de rigeur. Charging a client for time spent on bill review is a "nickel and dime" gesture which may provoke a client into becoming a former client.

13. **Get pre-approval for major expenses.** Get the client's approval for:

- out of town travel.
- retaining any outside experts or consultants.
- multiple adjusters at on-the-scene investigations, hearings and conferences.

Obtain advance approval for any obligations such as these. This could also avoid legal liability on the part of your adjusting firm. If you engage a contractor or vendor and the client balks at payment, the provider may look to you and you alone to satisfy the bill. This puts you in an uncomfortable situation, and adjusting companies get sued in such situations. Preferably, get it in writing any time the client authorizes you to retain an outside service provider. Next best is to write a letter to the client confirming the fact that they have given you such authority, and for them to let you know within a certain number of days if the letter does not reflect your mutual understanding.

Provide a Realistic Budget

A few comments about budgets in the context of individual claim files. While more and more law firms budget for cases they handle, the notion is slower in coming to the area of adjusting assignments. The adjusting company offering Cadillac service, however, will seize upon budgets as a way to deliver superior service at reasonable cost, and impress the client in the process. On the next page is a sample claim investigative plan and budget.

Some specific budgeting tips:

1. **Volunteer a budget.** Provide a budget to the client, even if not asked. When was the last time an adjusting firm ever provided a budget on one of its claim files? Chances are the answer is "never" or "rarely." Budgets are getting to be a fact of life among attorneys. Look for this trend to continue in the realm of the adjuster. More clients of law firms are requiring detailed written budgets on each case. As adjusting costs rise, this same request — or requirement — may be imposed upon outside claims adjusting outfits. Even if the client does not request a budget, the top-flight adjusting firm will likely impress the client by offering one anyway, unbidden.

2. **React quickly if budgets are requested.** If asked, provide

Claim Investigative Plan/Budget

Case _____   Claim No _____

	Activity Description	Adjuster	Time*	Estimated Expenses
Signed Statements				
Recorded Statements				
Photographs & Diagrams				
Reporting/ Correspondence				
Travel				
Phone Calls				
Negotiation				
Attorney Contact				
Miscellaneous**				
TOTAL				

* Please indicate hourly rate
** Please itemize

one promptly. Yes, I know that doing a budget is a pain in the posterior. On the fun scale, it ranks right up there with root canal therapy. No whining! Admittedly, a budget for a claim file is subject to a host of factors over which the adjuster has no control: new witnesses being identified, contacts from claimants and attorneys. The unexpected routinely crops up each work day in the claims department. Even given these caveats, it is a useful discipline.

Admittedly, not every claim file may warrant a budget. Large-scale investigations do, however, appear to be promising candidates. Further, any file where total billings are to exceed a certain figure, such as $1,000, may also be candidates. The format is less critical than the exercise and discipline of completing a budget.

Providing an unsolicited budget by an adjusting service also sends a positive message to the client. That message is, "We too are concerned about costs, will spend your money wisely, and are concerned about efficient claims-handling." However, clients may balk at paying for the time invested in preparing a budget, if they never requested one in the first place.

3. **Subject budgets to periodic tune-ups.** Update the budget periodically through the life of the case. Budgets should be dynamic, not static. Therefore, long-standing cases should have an updated budget at least once a year. For some cases, the adjuster may need to revise the budget even more frequently. If new investigative vistas open on what had been previously considered a narrow case, the claims rep should revise the budget upward. On the other hand, if certain investigative leads dry up — witnesses disappear, litigation prevents adjuster involvement, etc. — the budget may need to be revised downwards. The adjuster makes no guarantee with a budget that the adjusting fee will come in at this level. It is not a contract or a warranty. However, the adjuster should periodically compare the cumulative billings on a file to the budget, and either adjust the budget periodically or re-think her billing approach. Update budgets regularly, even if the client does not ask you to. It is a good habit. Make it a habit, and do them, unless the client explicitly asks you not to.

4. **Avoid exorbitant "fudge factors."** Avoid one of the oldest tricks in the book, i.e. calculating the time you think is needed and then adding a big "fudge factor." This will cause your budget to lose credibility. By all means, be conservative. Do not count on looking like a hero by coming in under a budget which was intentionally inflated to begin with.

5. **Remember the nickels and dimes.** Don't forget about expenses as a significant budget component. This includes mileage, photographs, tolls, photocopies, police and fire reports, medical report charges, fees for independent medical exams, air fare, meals, and lodging expense if overnight travel is planned, etc. These can add up. Factor them into the budget.

6. **Strive for realism.** Make the budget realistic. Ask yourself,

"If *I* were the client, what would I think of this budget?" Take some time with the budget. If you are not spending 45 minutes to an hour on the budget, you are probably not spending enough time.

7. **Appreciate the tie between budgets and reserves.** Budgets help the insurance client set realistic, accurate reserves. The cost to adjust a claim is a "transaction cost" which insurers and clients track. They cannot reserve for these costs accurately unless they have some way to estimate them. On a "micro" level, the individual claim file budget assists in this aim.

8. **Appreciate the link between budgets and intelligent case decisions.** Budgets help the insurance client make intelligent defend-or-settle decisions. If adjusting costs are going to be substantial, then a client might want to reconsider the wisdom of settlement. In many cases, the client will still opt for an investigation and claim defense. In either case, the client should be able to make such a decision based on facts — which budgets come close to providing — rather than mere supposition or conjecture.

9. **Get used to budgets.** They are a fact of life. In what other area does a customer have no idea —until the end — how much a service is going to cost? Granted, there are a few, but they are getting to be fewer and farther between. Lead the way. Set the standard. Offer to provide the client with a budget. Even if the client does not take you up on the offer, the mere fact that you asked will set you apart from the other 99 percent of all claim service providers.

Five Ways to Stay Within the Budget

Budgets do not operate on auto-pilot. Once the claims representative provides a client with an initial budget, there are a number of factors to consider. These include the following:

1. **Budgets are not etched in stone.** The budget is not a contractual guarantee. Resist any client attempt to put you in a box with regard to a budget. A budget should be your best educated guess as to how much in adjusting fees will be needed to see a claim file through to conclusion. Many insurers and self-insureds set reserves for allocated loss adjustment expenses (ALAE). One component of such expenses are adjusting fees. Thus, your good faith budget will help the client set expense reserves.

2. **Take budgets seriously, though.** Having said that, adjusters DO need to take budgets seriously. Just because the budget is not a guaranty or a contract does not mean that you should take it lightly. Just the opposite is true. You should make the budget realistic. To an extent, the client's financial condition may be impacted — positively or negatively — by the claim budget estimate and its reliability. Clients do not like surprises, but they are more apt to tolerate the surprise of you coming in under budget more than an unexpected over-budget variance.

3. **Act accountably.** Be prepared to explain any budget variance — over or under. If you are overbudget, offer the client an explanation for this. The discussion need not be brief. Were there unforeseen developments on the claim which required further work? Were there factors beyond the adjuster's control which drove expenses up? Were there extenuating circumstances? Review bills before they go out to clients. Compare the bills with your budget. If you are over budget, offer a brief explanation why. If you are underbudget, do not hesitate to point that out as well.

4. **Don't wait for a complaint to offer an explanation.** Provide such explanations preemptively, in advance of any client request for same. Do not wait for the client to complain. Anticipate client concerns over bills. If you have the remotest idea that the client will balk at a bill, provide a brief explanation with the bill to set the matter in some context.

5. **Put your budget in context.** Indicate whether the revised budget is global or incremental. Let's assume that your initial budget for handling a complex business interruption loss is $750. Six months later the file is still open, so you submit a revised budget of $1,250. Is this $1,250 all-inclusive, or is it over and above the $750 you had already estimated? This makes a big monetary difference for the client. The client may believe that the $1,250 figure is all-inclusive. If the adjuster views it as incremental, that would bring the total adjusting bill to $2,000 ($750 + $1,250). This is almost a tripling of the original bill. Thus, to avoid giving the client nasty surprises or prevent deterioration in client trust, make it clear whether any revised/interim budget is incremental or all-inclusive.

How To Save Clients Money in Travel Costs

Runaway travel expenses are one way to irritate clients on the cost side of the ledger. By contrast, showing some thought and frugality when it comes to travel costs will impress clients in a favorable way. When you embark on out of town travel on a case, clear such travel ahead of time with the client. This may avoid problems down the road when you go to get your bill paid and the client wants to know who authorized the trip. Use common sense here. Unless the trip is an emergency where you do not have the chance to seek clearance, seek such clearance.

Another way is to present the client with a "negative option." Book and record clubs are known for this. Advise the client that you need to take the trip for whatever reason. Tell them that unless you hear from them to the contrary within X number of days, you will infer that you have their blessing for the trip. This is one way around the bureaucratic delays which, unfortunately, insurance and claim departments often have.

Before you board the plane for that get-acquainted meeting with the insured 1,200 miles away, before camping in the client's corporate headquarters for a week reviewing internal documents, you had best get that travel approved in advance or at least notify the client clearly up front that such travel is necessary. Some other suggestions for the frugal traveller:

1. **Fly coach.** If you want to fly first class, pay the difference yourself. Most insurance company employees — and often this includes the executives — never fly first class except at their own expense. You want to convey the appearance — as well as reality — of frugality. Fly coach.

2. **Book your travel arrangements well in advance to save your client the most money.** Non-refundable tickets often have the lowest price. Work with an experienced travel agent to learn the best ways to save on air fares.

3. **Consider Saturday stay-overs.** Frequently, the additional lodging expense will be more than offset by the savings in air fare. Frequently, there is a dramatic drop in ticket price when one stays over a Saturday night.

4. **Consider taking the train.** Train fares are cheaper, if the distance is manageable. Often, you can get a roomette, plug in your laptop computer and get lots of work done. When you get hungry, you can walk down to the dining car and eat off of real plates instead of airplane trays. You get more room to get up, stretch and move about. For those who have a "fear of flying," going by train may be an efficient alternative with savings translatable to the clients.

5. **Try not to accomplish just one task on any trip.** Try to cluster work from a number of different assignments on one trip as much as possible. Pro-rate the time and expenses to each client. Clients are often concerned that when lawyers work for more than one client on a trip, that the full time of the trip will be charged to each client instead of enjoying the benefits of pro-rated expenses. Consider the remarks of James Gordon, law professor at Brigham Young University (*Washington Post*, 7/7/91, "Secrets of the Bar"):

> *"Ask how many hours associates are required to bill. In some firms, associates bill as many as 3,000 hours a year. Sometimes this is accomplished through "triple billing," a technique by which an*

169

> *associate works on client A's matter while flying to*
> *a city for client B, and he thinks that the issue may*
> *possibly be somehow someday relevant to client C.*
> *So he bills each client full bore."*

Needless to say, clients object to "triple billing." It should also go without saying that lodging in concierge-level hotels and billing meals in five-star restaurants will not impress the insurance client. This does not mean that insurers expect their attorneys to stay at the Bates Motel and dine on Big Macs. Some middle road is possible and even economical.

For most adjusters on overnight business travel, the hotel is simply a place to shower and sleep. Debbie Fields, magnate of Mrs. Fields Cookies, flies coach and lodges at $50-a-night Hampton Inns. She figures the savings is better spent on business development and management bonuses. Be frugal when travelling on the client's tab. If you want to watch in-room movies on Spectravision and munch from the honor bar, that's fine. Just don't put that on the client's tab.

If you travel in an ostentatious style, consider what this is telling the client about your adjusting practice, thrift and cost-consciousness. No client wants to get the impression that their service providers are living "high off the hog" at the client's expense. Be prepared to pay the difference.

How to Handle
a Billing Complaint

Make sure adjusting bills are fair, prompt and user-friendly. Make sure that your fees meet the client's expectations, budget guidelines and timetables. To do this effectively, you need to discuss these sensitive issues at the beginning of an assignment or at the outset of establishing account guidelines. Determine in advance how detailed your clients expect your bills to be, and when in doubt, err on the side of caution and additional detail. Many clients want an itemized list of the cost of each service performed. Try to follow such preferences whenever possible.

Even with the utmost care, adjusting companies may receive a bill complaint from time to time. (There are some managers who sincerely believe that, if they aren't receiving an occasional bill complaint, then they probably are not charging ENOUGH!) Some tips on dealing with and handling the bill complaint so as to not lose a client:

1. **Acknowledge the complaint immediately.** Before the sun sets that day, at least send the client a brief confirming note. This letter should convey some of these things:

- Acknowledge that you have received the complaint.
- That you take this very seriously and value them as a client.
- That you will carefully review the bill.

- You promise a more complete response within a certain number of days, preferably no more than 30.

2. **Review the file, and do not bill the client for the review.** Spend some time reviewing the file. Shut off the phone and cloister yourself against interruptions for thirty minutes or an hour, if you must. In your judgment, does the client have a legitimate gripe? Are there extenuating circumstances of which the client is unaware? Take notes as you review the file.

3. **Have the handling adjuster review the file and complete a legible bill itemization sheet.** In some cases, it may help to also have the adjuster provide a brief written explanation about those bill charges or entries in question. Try to get the client focused on what part of the bill causes him indigestion.

The hardest bill complaint to address is the amorphous, "This bill is too high." Try to pin the client down, as diplomatically as possible, as to what specific part of the bill is objectionable. Ask the adjuster to review the file and comment. Ask the adjuster to write or dictate a synopsis or explanation. Caution the adjuster that this should be something which can — at your option — be sent to the client. No blowing off steam at the client or venting one's spleen because you think the client is a penny-pinching whiner.

4. **Provide a substantive point-by-point response to the client's complaint.** Explain why the charges were reasonable for each entry. Ask the adjuster who handled the file to provide an explanation.

5. **Don't get defensive.** Resist the temptation to unload on the client. There may be some clients who complain inordinately about bills. After a while, the adjusting service must ask itself if it really wants such a client. Is the aggravation worth it?

6. **Admit inefficiencies.** Some areas of billing are judgment calls. These calls should go in the client's favor as much as possible. If you as a supervisor or examiner feel that the file could have been handled more efficiently, if there was some wheel-spinning, then graciously admit it. That does NOT mean that

you have to admit it was intentional. It does mean that sometimes well-meaning claims people can be "heavy" on time charges.

7. **Identify any legitimate work for which the client was not charged.** Perhaps the adjuster could have charged for some tasks which were not billed: waiting time in a lawyer's office while "cooling heels," trying to locate a paramedic to question him about a fire's origin, etc. It is always best, however, to identify these briefly in advance of the bill complaint. To dredge these up after the client has complained may appear less than credible and too contrived. Still, if you can make a strong case, do so and you might be able to blunt some criticism.

8. **Offer to write down the bill.** Be open to negotiation. Do not get pig-headed. Getting paid for part of the bill is better than getting stiffed, or having the payment held up. Gently suggest to the client that they pay the undisputed portion of the bill, while the two of you continue discussions regarding the charges in question. This at least benefits your cash flow. If the client insists on holding the undisputed part of the bill hostage to the disputed part, reconsider whether this is the kind of client you want or need for your business growth. As much as everyone wants to keep clients happy, there may be times when you make a conscious decision to "fire" or let go a client. If they are being absolutely unreasonable about a bill, if they expect something for nothing, then you may improve your business's health by letting such a client walk and chalking the episode up to experience.

9. **Cut the bill.** If the client has caught a bill with problems, or if it is a gray area, voluntarily cut the bill. You may reduce your billing in the short run, but you keep a client happy in the long run. The latter is a more significant determinant of your ability to succeed in business as an independent adjusting service.

10. **Provide client with an "action plan" as to why the problem will not recur.** If the client has questioned some egregious billing practice, propose an action plan of steps you have taken within the adjusting service to prevent future transgressions.

This could include spot audits of time sheets with files, closer scrutiny of service bills before they go to the client, reducing billing/production quotas for certain adjusters, etc.

11. **Avoid "surprise" billings.** For example, if a bill is going to be significantly higher than originally estimated, alert clients to this before you send the bill. The same advice applies to work which is going to be delayed.

Research

Your client hired you (presumably, hopefully?) because of your expertise in a particular field of claims adjusting. Thus, many clients see red when they review adjusting fee bills and spot entries for "research." This bill entry has a tendency to trigger alarm bells. Let's just say that this is a category susceptible to spinning out of control. Some clients may have been burned by situations where they felt some young adjuster was parked in a library and went crazy on a research project, treating it like a brief to the Supreme Court.

A few cynical clients feel that adjusting firms, in the marketing stage, emphasize their familiarity with an area of adjusting work, only to invariably need to research it once they are given assignments. Additionally, many clients look askance at being billed for research which they think amounts to paying for your or your trainee's OJT.

Doubtlessly there are arcane areas of adjusting procedure and practice which a particular claim might present. No one seriously argues that, once you finish your initial training program as an adjuster, you never need to crack another book. Research is occasionally needed to shore up a defense, support a theory you have, or understand some turgid medical records. In that case, explain beforehand the need for such research to the client. Do NOT follow the adage that "It's better to seek forgiveness than to ask permission." Make your case briefly and succinctly to the client and you may avoid billing challenges and hard feelings.

Better yet, go one step further. Detail not only the reason for the research, but also indicate:

- How long, in number of hours, the research will take.
- Who will do the research.
- The hourly rate at which the research time will be charged.
- Whether any of the research will be computerized.

Give the client some lead time, if at all possible, for deciding to give the green or red light on your research project. In some circumstances, you may not have the luxury of much time for making a decision. In this case, use your best judgment. You do not have the luxury of a lot of prior consultation. No client should second-guess you in a situation like this. These situations are the exception and not the rule, though.

A nice touch is to make sure you give the client a hard copy of your research work product. If the issue is a recurring one for the client, this investment may be beneficial to other cases, pending or future.

Another way to approach the research authorization is by using what I call the "negative option." Book- and record clubs use this extensively. Simply outline the need for research to the client and state something to the effect that, "If I do not hear from you to the contrary within XX [pick a reasonable time frame], I will assume I have authority to proceed with this proposed research." Caution: Get to know the client a while before you attempt something like this, or the client may find it presumptuous.

If there is any question in your mind, ask the client up front about research. Needless to say, if the client has written guidelines requiring pre-authorization of research projects, abide by that stipulation. If you forget, be prepared to eat part of the bill. In this case, it truly is easier to seek permission than forgiveness.

Statements

Ask yourself honestly, "Do we REALLY need to take this statement?" Be selective, unless the client absolutely insists on a particular statement. There may be some cases where a statement will likely make no difference one way or the other to the client's defense. In such an instance, consider foregoing a statement or perhaps, with prior notice, obtaining an interview instead or sending a lower-priced adjuster for some "teeth-cutting" experience.

Are there some statements which you do not need?

Provide "executive summaries" of statements in lieu of a transcript, a blow-by-blow or multi-page description. I know of few insurance claim reps who have the time to read an entire recorded statement transcript. Many "summaries" hardly are worthy of the name, and are still much too lengthy. Some clients may differ.

Instead of billing for taking a statement, then billing the client to provide a multi-page statement summary which may not be read either, consider giving a two page (maximum) executive summary. Focus on the bottom line: most clients simply want to know, "Did the statement help, hurt or have no effect on the defensibility of my case?" Answer this question straight-up at the beginning, and embellish later. Start at the conclusion, and if the client wants a blow-by-blow description or a verbatim transcript, by all means provide one.

Don't Reassign
Your Client's Work

Insurance clients seek accountability for their work. One pet peeve of many insurance clients is the tendency of some adjusting companies and offices to treat the client's case like a hot potato. The client assigns a case to a senior adjuster … initially. Three months later, the file is reassigned to an intermediate level adjuster. Then, later, a one-year adjuster. Then, maybe, an adjuster trainee.

Each one, of course, must become familiar with the file. And that takes time, of course. In legal services, time is money. Not the firm's money, the client's.

Trips down the letterhead annoy clients. For some reason though, the trips never seem to go *up* the letterhead.

It also galls the client that a senior rainmaker type does the courting of a client. Thereafter, once the tap (and assignments) starts to flow, the rainmaker is never seen or heard-from again. This often prompts the client to ask, "Hey, where'd my rainmaker go?"

Turnover of key account personnel within adjusting firms is an anathema to all clients.

It creates the impression that the client's file is a commodity, a fungible item. A case is a case is a case. It implies an assembly-line approach to case-handling. No client finds this a flattering inference.

Moreover, adjusters should be aware that it risks sending a disturbing message to the client about the claims profession. At a time when adjusters are struggling to build their image as professionals, the reassignment of case from adjuster to adjuster carries a meta-message that one adjuster is as good as another. Clients know otherwise, however.

Adjusters working for insurance carriers or self-insureds should realize that they are in the personal services business. Plugging in different adjusters into a case carries the impression as well that claim services are commodities.

Some adjusting firms may be enamored with the "team approach" to claim defense and case-handling. Many concoct elaborate and half-convincing arguments as to how this will actually *save* client's money. Maybe so, but expect some client skepticism. Reassigning a case or team-staffing a case creates many concerns on the client's part:

- Increased cost from having each adjuster get up to speed on a file.
- Increased costs from having more charges for inter-office conferences.
- Lack of accountability, since the client is not sure who really is in charge or most familiar with the case.
- Lack of interest on the adjusting firm's part. The insurance client is concerned that its cases will become the orphan stepchild, shuffled from one person to another.

In all, the adjusting service may be more in love with the team approach than are their clients. However, many clients agree in principle with the notion that, in order to save costs, a case's handling should be delegated downward to its lowest appropriate level. If this means an adjuster with a lower hourly rate, the client — theoretically — captures some savings.

Theoretically.

The theory can break down in practice, however. By itself,

hourly rate can be a misleading index of cost. Cost is a function of hourly rate times the number of hours. The problem arises when the "cheaper" adjuster with the lower hourly rate takes twice as much time to complete a task due to inexperience, lack of supervision or zeal to meet the monthly billing quota. Sometimes an apparent deal is no deal at all.

There are situations where it makes sense to reassign a file from one adjuster to another. There are situations where a team approach is appropriate to case defense. Rather than presume that clients are agreeable to this, however, talk it over with the client beforehand. This can avoid friction and misunderstandings. Adjusters will learn that, in this context, it is easier to seek permission than to present the client with an accomplished fact.

Turnover of key account personnel drives (insurance) clients nuts. Avoid it if you can, and you will keep clients happy. You will also be doing your part to professionalize the claims industry. Interchangeable adjusters send the message that adjusters are commodities. That is not the kind of impression conveyed by adjusting services who wish to keep clients happy.

The Service "Extras"

S ometimes it's the extras which make a difference, whether it's in buying a car or retaining an adjusting service. Perhaps we define our business too narrowly when we say we are in the claims adjusting business. We are really in the problem-solving business. Clients find claims troublesome. It is up to us to make the experience as smooth, painless and trouble-free as possible.

In this section, you will learn about three examples of ways that claim departments and services can "go the extra mile" for their clients. This is by no means an exhaustive list, and readers should view these as starting — not ending — points for the question, "What more can we do for clients which adds value to our service?"

Offer an Expert
Witness Database

Risk and claim managers realize that winning or losing cases — in court or at the negotiation stage — often turns on a battle of the experts. Metallurgists, economists, accident reconstructionists — the risk and claims manager needs them all from time to time. Too often, claim professionals relegate these decisions to the defense lawyer. Perhaps it's because they are too busy. Maybe it's because they do not see the payoff from getting involved. Possibly they presume greater expertise on the defense lawyer's part than is warranted. For whatever reason, "Let defense counsel do it," becomes the spoken or subtle motto. This is unwise. Claim professionals can save their companies or clients money and boost the chances of successful defense by observing and practicing the following:

1. **Get involved in picking experts.** Do NOT delegate this to counsel. By all means, seek counsel's input on recommended experts. An attorney's ties to a community of experts is a plus that selected firms can bring to the table. Experts are too expensive — and too vital to case defense — to leave this function to defense attorneys, who have no financial accountability for the consequences. That does not mean you should neuter defense counsel when it comes to making recommendations, though.

2. **Establish written cost parameters and authorization requirements.** Adjusters should require that counsel provide the following information before retaining any outside expert or consultant:

- a copy of the expert/consultant's resume or curriculum vita (c.v.).
- the expert's hourly rate.
- the nature and scope of the retention, including whether the expert will function as a behind-the-scenes consultant or as a trial witness.
- a rough approximation of the number of hours the expert/consultant will need.

Without this information, the claims person should return back to the defense attorney any request for authorization. This information is essential in order to evaluate and reserve each case. Retention of experts can send expense reserves sky-high. Such projected costs may also cast settlement in a very different, more appealing light.

This also avoids unpleasant surprises. Recently our company tried a case, retaining a much-needed expert. After the deposition of our chief defense expert, distraught defense counsel phoned the examiner. Dr. Expert had billed at $300 from portal to portal, including billing us for the time he spent sleeping. First class travel. A suite at the San Francisco Four Seasons Clift. The good doctor faxed the bill to the defense attorney, probably within 30 minutes after arriving back home in Philadelphia. Moral: Develop written cost guidelines. Of course, sometimes a particular witness is so essential and key to your case that you would gladly treat him like a pampered pasha if it means retaining his time, expertise and good will.

A pet peeve many claims professionals have about some defense attorneys is the types of decisions they expect you to make on the basis of very scant information. For example, our company has written guidelines which incorporate the preceding requirements. Yet, invariably, we still receive umpteen urgent requests from defense counsel, needing authority to retain this expert or that. No discussion of hourly fees. No discussion about the scope of the expert's assignment or range of hours needed to complete this task. We — the client — are now in the position of having to follow up with counsel to request that which we've already asked for once in our written guidelines. This wastes time, money and betrays an inattentiveness on counsel's part in reading our guidelines. (What ELSE is counsel ignoring?) Written guidelines are a good start, but the client must continually "preach the gospel" to outside counsel to make sure they understand.

3. **Don't overlook in-house experts.** Do not reinvent the wheel. There may be people inside the client's own company who would make superb witnesses at trial. They are well-credentialed and present nicely to a jury. Handicap number one is their perceived lack of objectivity, since they are employees of the defendant. On the other hand, one school of thought is that juries nowadays recognize that everyone on the witness stand is "hired" in one sense or another.

There are dangers as well in NOT having an inside expert testify, especially in a product liability case. Forgoing an in-house expert can leave a bad impression on a jury and create an opening for plaintiff's counsel to exploit: "See, they think so little of their product, ladies and gentlemen of the jury, that they had to go far outside the company and hire someone to try to defend their Whizmoo 700 machine. Not a single person within the company could be persuaded to get up here and defend their own product ... !"

4. **Require counsel to be specific when they request authority for retaining experts.** Too often, defense lawyers ask clients and insurers to make significant financial commitments without providing enough information needed to make an intelligent decision. Tell lawyers that before authorizing retention of any expert they must provide you with:

- the expert's c.v.

- hourly rate.
- whether the expert will function as a consultant or as a testifying expert.
- the general range, scope or number of hours the expert needs to complete the project.

Make it clear to outside counsel: No information — no authorization.

5. **Develop a database of expert witnesses and consultants.** Proactive claim service companies will often learn that the same experts come up against them in certain cases time after time. Similarly, certain defense experts may be superb on many different cases, though one should guard against using the same expert all the time. Save time, aggravation and maybe even money by developing a list of experts — defense AND plaintiff. This can be computerized but doesn't necessarily have to be so. It can be in a file drawer. Periodically update this registry as well.

It should include about each expert: copy of the curriculum vita, fee schedule, address, phone and fax number, area of specialization, academic background, references, academic degrees and a general comments section.

6. **Cultivate contacts and dig your well before you're thirsty.** The time to seek experts is before you get sued. For many companies, that may seem extreme. Companies do contingency planning for a host of events — property loss, establishing credit lines for tight times, planning corporate succession, etc. Somehow, when it comes to preparing for lawsuits, no one wants to plan. This is somewhat understandable, since preparing for lawsuits is sort of like planning your own funeral: despite its inevitability, it's uncomfortable to contemplate. Each company knows or should know of experts in their fields. Adjusting firms should maintain current panels of good independent medical examination (IME) physicians in their area. The same with accident reconstruction experts. Hospitals, or companies insuring them should collect names, leads and resumes of experts in areas from aseptic reactions to zygomatic arch replacements.

185

7. **Beware of eggheads.** There are plenty of multi-degreed, super credentialed academicians who simply cannot communicate with a jury. Make sure that if you do get an egghead, you get an egghead who:

- has strong verbal communication skills.
- can explain technical subjects in ways intelligible to lay persons.
- "projects to the jury" as a believable and likeable individual.

Admittedly subjective as these factors are, they must nevertheless weigh alongside the more tangible stack of sheepskins.

8. **Avoid "whores."** Pardon my French. Avoid "hired gun" experts who derive most of their income from testifying or preparing to testify, or who profess to be experts in everything from cranes to Coke bottle explosions. You can get an expert and, for a suitable fee, you can probably get an expert who will say anything. Take a look at the back of magazines such as *Trial* (the mouthpiece of the plaintiff's bar) or even the *ABA Journal.*

The proliferation of "junk science" is so monstrous that recently the defense bar, through organizations such as the Defense Research Institute (DRI), now combats the parade of unqualified plaintiff experts. Presumably, the effort should also extend to purging from the defense ranks equally tainted experts.

9. **Beware of advertisers.** Pick up any legal trade magazine today — *Trial* magazine or the *ABA Journal,* and you are likely to find long lists of experts to consult and testify on everything from shopping center security to cancer-phobia. These classifieds have supplanted the "personals" column. In general, avoid the advertisers unless they are the only dog in the kennel. The fact that they advertise may undermine their credibility in front of a jury. It may also indicate that they derive much of their income not from practicing their trade but from serving as an expert witness. It reinforces the image of hired gun, which often does not sit well with juries.

10. **Remember the little touches.** Establish the groundwork

for a long-term relationship with a very effective expert. This may include making sure that you pay his bill on time! It may involve writing him a brief note thanking him for his help. Little touches like this might make the difference two years later when you desperately need the expert again, and you find his Day-Timer booked solid with other priorities.

The claim examiner preparing for trial is like a movie director: you select a theme, develop a story, line up the "actors" and rehearse the script. The defense lawyer plays a large role, but the defense lawyer is often not sensitive to certain cost considerations and may have no "feel" for where to look for experts. With the preceding guidelines, claim professionals can seek the best of both worlds, controlling costs and maximizing results as the big show prepares for trial. Lowers costs and effective preparation keeps clients happy.

Check Your "Litigation Management IQ"

When it comes to litigation management, many claim departments, adjusting companies and third-party administrators "talk the talk." But do they "walk the walk"? Effective litigation management can add an extra dimension to your claim service. It provides you with a competitive advantage and allows you to keep clients happy by managing costs and avoiding nasty surprises.

Here is a self-diagnostic tool to determine if litigation management is substance or lip service:

		YES	NO
1.	Do you comparison-shop for defense lawyers?	___	___
2.	Do your attorneys only do work that adjusters cannot perform?	___	___
3.	Do you require detailed budgets at the outset, with periodic updates?	___	___
4.	Do you require lawyers to report at specific time intervals?	___	___
5.	Do you give written service standards to counsel at the assignment stage?	___	___
6.	Are bills itemized by task, in tenth-of-an-hour increments?	___	___

	YES	NO
7. Do you have an "early warning system" for accumulating legal fees?	—	—
8. Do you audit — not rubber-stamp — outside legal bills?	—	—
9. Have you questioned a legal bill within the last 90 days?	—	—
10. Must legal research undertaken on your behalf be approved in advance?	—	—

Score: Give yourself one point for each "yes" answer; zero for "no." **9-10:** You are a pro at litigation management! **7-8:** You're headed in the right direction, but may want to fine-tune your tactics. **5-6:** Beware of babysitting files passively instead of managing them. **0-4:** You may need an accountant, or a bankruptcy attorney, not a liability defense lawyer!

Effective litigation management may be one large unmet need waiting to be fulfilled by adjusting companies. Charlie Caronia of Caronia Corporation states that, "TPA's as a whole are not aggressive in claims management. Too often, TPA's are simply paper conduits for outside counsel, especially on flat-fee arrangements" He adds, "TPA's are controlled by counsel when it should be just the other way around." Too often, Caronia feels, a vague complaint is followed by a vague answer filed by outside counsel. This is a prescription for delay and high costs. "Somebody has to pick up the phone," Caronia states, "and ask, 'What is the allegation?' 'What is your theory of liability?' 'What is your realistic demand in this case?'"

Interrogatory Assistance

Despite the adjuster's best efforts, sometimes claims go into litigation. At this point, the insured will often have to provide written answers to questions from the other (plaintiff's) side. These written questions are called "interrogatories." Usually the defense attorney takes the lead role in fashioning responses to interrogatories.

Frequently, the interrogatories ask questions about the defendant's insurance coverage: effective dates, policy limits, name of carrier, any coverage issues, etc. On these insurance-related points, the adjuster may be the most well-versed. Sometimes the adjuster works hand-in-hand with defense counsel in preparing answers to interrogatories. When this happens, there are ways to make the client happy and ways to annoy the client.

First and foremost, give the client plenty of lead time in answering interrogatories. This is common courtesy but also good claims practice and business sense. Few thing irritate clients as much as being placed under the gun because an adjuster (or an attorney) took his or her sweet time in submitting the interrogatories.

This pertains as well to interrogatories related to insurance coverage. More and more, it seems, plaintiffs are seeking insurance information through discovery, and getting it. True story: A few years ago a young associate attorney from a Wichita, Kansas law firm phoned me, frantic. This was at 4:45 p.m. on a Thursday, immediately preceding a Memorial Day holiday. Breathlessly, she stated that she needed insurance policy information AND a copy of the insurance policy ASAP to answer some interrogatories which were due. She needed these the following morning. I inquired as to how long she had known that this coverage information would be needed. Three weeks, she replied meekly. Needless to say, this did not sit well with me, and I took it up with a partner at the defense firm. It slipped the attorney's mind and, as a result, some other busy person (namely, the client) must scramble around, under time pressure, jumping through hoops for a law firm which is supposed to be a service provider. Unfortunately, obtaining insurance information is often number 17 on the attorney's "To Do" list. As a result, clients often resent being put under the gun, in a time-bind, because of someone else's procrastination.

Clients will appreciate it if they receive as much lead time as possible in answering interrogatories. In fact, it is a good practice to send the interrogatories to clients as soon as you receive them. Well, adjusters do not practice law. In fact, unauthorized practice of law by lay adjusters can land a claims professional in hot water. Isn't this a consideration for outside defense counsel rather than for an adjusting firm? The answer is, yes and no.

If adjusting firms or third-party administrators are in charge of litigation management for clients, there are some service guidelines they can establish to keep clients mollified. Require, for example, that outside counsel draft proposed answers to interrogatories for the client. This is a convenience for the client. Obviously, the client has the final say, but a good lawyer can help clients immeasurably by suggesting draft answers and then reviewing them with the client. A good TPA can require that outside counsel help out in this manner.

The TPA can also require that outside counsel send interrogatories to the client on the same day that counsel receives them. This gives clients maximum lead-time in fashioning responses. Make sure that clients know the due date for interrogatory answers.

Most clients are not happy about being involved in litigation. There are ways to handle interrogatories, though, that will prevent clients from being further aggravated and to make the "discovery" process as painless as possible.

Conclusion

Let's conclude where we began. It is much easier to talk — and write — about client service than to deliver it. This is particularly true in the field of claims and loss adjustment. Staffing shortages, exploding caseloads, hard-boiled cynicism and short-sighted procedures often make it difficult for any of us to put the client first. It is easy to be so focused on the "trees" of individual file handling that we lose sight of the "forest" of client satisfaction. Whether you define your client as the risk manager, insurance carrier or policyholder (or all of the above), the ideas discussed here should help us all raise not only our consciousness but also our performance.

Just reading about it will not do the job, however. Claim professionals must *do*, not just read. The success of these ideas comes with their application, not discussion. Those individuals and companies who adopt the Nike motto and "Just do it" will succeed in raising their level of client service, satisfaction and — a nice by-product here — their profits. Firms which attain the "gold standard" of service are those who have a bias for action, for doing, for trying new things, even if some of them don't work or fit well.

This discussion does not denigrate the importance of technical adjusting ability as a way to keep clients happy. Clients take it as a given, however, that firms holding themselves out as professional adjusting firms are technically competent. Without such expertise, all of the ideas in this book and an entire bookshelf will not placate a client. The substance of technical claims-adjusting prowess must be there. No amount of frills, gloss or a "menu of services" can compensate for an adjuster who cannot cover the important elements of a signed statement or who lacks perseverance in tracking down that hard-to-find witness.

Another positive by-product is that, by becoming obsessed with client service, we can all raise the image of the claims adjusting profession in the eyes of the lay public. I do not suggest that we undertake these ideas as an elaborate P.R. job, only that if you change reality, the perceptions will come around and improve.

If you've gotten this far, you have *read*.

Now, it's time to *do*.

Good luck and good service!

Selected Resource Readings on Client Service

There are many, many books about customer service, but the following are my personal favorites. They have nothing to do with insurance or claims, and everything to do with insurance and claims. Each tells a story about customer and client service which is worthy of our attention and application.

Brinkerhoff, John, *101 Commonsense Rules for the Office*, Stackpole Books, 1992.

Donnelly, James H., *Close to the Customer: 25 Management Tips From the Other Side of the Counter*, Business One Irwin, 1992.

Glen, Peter *It's Not My Department!: How to Get the Service You What, Exactly the Way You Want It!*, William Morrow and Company, Inc., 1990.

Mackay, Harvey, *Beware the Naked Man Who Offers You His Shirt*, William Morrow and Company, Inc., 1990.

Ibid., Swim With The Sharks, Without Getting Eaten Alive, Ivy Books, 1988.

McCormack, Mark H., *What They Don't Teach You at Harvard Business School*, Bantam Books, 1984.

McCormack, Mark H., *The 110% Solution*, Villard Books, 1991.

Peters, Thomas and Waterman, Robert, *In Search of Excellence:*

Lessons From America's Best-Run Companies, Harper & Row, 1982.

Poppe, Fred, *50 Rules to Keep a Client Happy*, Harper & Row, 1987.

Sewell, Carl and Brown, Paul, *Customers For Life: How to Turn That One-Time Buyer Into a Lifetime Customer*, Simon & Schuster, 1990.

Whiteley, Richard C., *The Customer Driven Company: Moving From Talk to Action*, Addison-Wesley, 1991.

Reader's Survey

As the reader of this book, you are *my* customer. Please take a few minutes to let me know whether this book has met or exceeded your expectations. No more than five minutes is needed to complete this survey.

Please answer the questions below. (Photocopy the pages if you wish.) Select the number on a scale of 1 (strongly disagree) to 7 (strongly agree) that best reflects your response to the question.

1. The words in this book are at a level appropriate for readers with my education and background.
       1   2   3   4   5   6   7

2. The book is organized in a way that makes it easy for me to find the information I need.
       1   2   3   4   5   6   7

3. The book's tone is just about right: not too academic nor too casual.
       1   2   3   4   5   6   7

4. The anecdotes and examples illustrate the points that are being made.
       1   2   3   4   5   6   7

5. This book includes much information that is new to me.
       1   2   3   4   5   6   7

6. I believe I can apply ideas from this book to my work.
       1   2   3   4   5   6   7

7. I expect to continue to use this book as a reference or source of ideas.
       1   2   3   4   5   6   7

8. I have recommended this book to others, or probably will.
       1   2   3   4   5   6   7

9. Please indicate the extent to which this book has met your expectations overall.
       1   2   3   4   5   6   7

10. Please describe how you will apply the information in this book to your work situation.

_____

_____

_____

11. Please tell me at least one thing that would make this book more useful to you.

_____

_____

_____

Please send your completed survey to:
Kevin M. Quinley
MEDMARC Insurance Company
P.O. Box 1167
Fairfax, VA 22030-1677
Thank you!

about the author

Kevin M. Quinley is Vice President of Risk Services for MEDMARC Insurance Company and Hamilton Resources Corporation, Fairfax, Virginia. A graduate of Wake Forest University (BA) and the College of William & Mary (MA), he holds the Chartered Property & Casualty Underwriter (CPCU) designation and specialty designations from the Insurance Institute of America in Risk Management (ARM), in Claims (AIC) and in Management (AIM).

He is a Contributing Editor of both *Claims* and *Medical Device & Diagnostic Industry* magazine. The author of over 125 published articles, his writings have appeared in *Business Insurance, Risk Management, Rough Notes, Best's Review, CPCU Journal, Insurance Settlement Journal* and *For the Defense*. His two prior books are *Time Management for Claim Professionals* and *Claims Management: How to Select, Manage and Save Money on Adjusting Services.*

He teaches classes in insurance, claims and risk management for the Washington D.C. Chapter of the Society of CPCU, for which he served as President in 1992. A member of the Risk and Insurance Managers' Society (RIMS) and the American Society of Health Care Risk Management, he is a frequent writer and speaker on topics relating to risk- and litigation management. He lives with his wife and two sons in Fairfax, Virginia.